Able to Cook

A 30th Anniversary Celebration

Scented Rose Geranium Cake

Able Community Care

Celebrating 30 Years of Care

Able to Cook

First published in Great Britain in July 2010 by Able Community Care

Able Community Care
The Old Parish Rooms
Whitlingham Lane
Trowse,
Norwich NR14 8TZ
Tel 01603 764567
www.uk-care.com

ISBN 978-1-903571-94-1

A CIP catalogue record for this book is available from the British Library

Edited by Fran Glendining
Design by Brendan Rallison
Printed by Colour Print Ltd

Thank you to all our contributors who generously
provided recipes and donations.

Photographs:
The photographs used throughout this book are representative.

The following photos were contributed by:
Cover photo: Hand with Eggs © Cati Majtenyi
Back cover: Basket of Grapes © Cati Majtenyi
Scented Rose Geranium Cake: © Nicole Rowntree
Bread, cheese and pickles : © Piers Warren
Photo montages include contributions from Brendan Rallison, Fran Glendining,
Phill Coe, Piers Warren, Denise Ames and Lucille Bartlam.

Foreword

Thirty years ago a telephone call to a small company in Norfolk formed a fledgling idea which has grown to be of benefit to thousands of older and disabled people throughout the United Kingdom.

The idea led to the beginning of Able Community Care which gives choice to people who, despite having the needs for care services twenty four hours a day, wish to remain living in their own homes, within their own communities and surrounded by the memories, objects and choices that have made up the fabric of their lives.

Able Community Care specialises in the provision of continuous, live-in, housekeeper/carer schemes which are available in England, Scotland, Wales and The Channel Islands..

Working in the world of people's lives, the practical side of life is always there and what could be more practical than having the food of choice prepared and served to you in your own home when you are no longer able to do it for yourself. Over the years many recipes had been passed down to us from care workers and our clients and when the idea came as to how we could celebrate our 'pearl' anniversary, a cookery book made up of our care workers and clients dishes came to mind.

Ideas grow and soon the notion of putting together a commercial cookery book, one where all the profits would be donated to charities was born. Add to the mix the idea of writing to celebrities to ask if they would donate a recipe and the "die was cast"

The result is a cookery book containing recipes from people closely connected to Able Community Care, from celebrities with links to Norfolk, and stories and comments to add to the blend.

Enjoy making the dishes printed on these pages and thank you for helping raise funds for Age UK Norfolk and Connects & Co.

Angela Gifford

Proprietor of Able Community Care since 1980

Contents

Soups, Snacks and Starters

Mains

Chicken

Chicken Breasts in Cream and Pernod Sauce	*Bill Treacher*	41
Chicken Balti	*Anna Lucas and BJ Cole*	42
Chicken Curry	*Nigel Worthington*	43
Chicken Josephine	*Jo Kydd*	44
Chicken Matilda	*Councillor Evelyn Collishaw*	45
Garlic and Herb Chicken	*David Whiteley and Amelia Reynolds*	46
Garlic and Lemon Chicken	*Susannah York*	47
Marinated Chicken with Vegetables	*Fiona Bruce*	48
Very Quick Pesto Chicken	*Libby Purves OBE*	48
Summer Chicken Salad	*Rt Hon Sir John Major KG CH*	49
Spice-Roasted Chicken	*Carrick's at Castle Farm*	50

Fish

Alison's Pasta	*Alison Schofield*	51
Baked Salmon in Filo Parcels	*Susie Fowler-Watt*	52
Char-Grilled Fish With Summer Salsa Salad	*Deb Jordan*	53
Coda di Rospo Alla Livornese	*Viscountess Knollys OBE DL*	54
Freshwater Crayfish	*John Wilson MBE*	55
Fricassée of Smoked Haddock	*Peter Bowles*	56
Paella Paradise	*Matthew Brewin*	57
Prawn Spag	*Norman Lamb MP*	58
Salmon Fillet with Parmesan Crust	*Colonel Mark Cook OBE*	59
Trout with Almonds	*Prunella Scales CBE*	59
Shrimp/Prawn Gumbo	*Nikki Banham*	60
Swordfish Mexicali	*Joan Armstrong*	61
Zarzuella	*Iestyn Thomas*	62

Game

Congham Pigeon Breasts in Red Wine	*Henry Bellingham MP*	64
Pheasant with Lime and Ginger	*Sir Nicholas and Lady Bacon*	64
Kentish Hot Rabbit Casserole	*Frederick Forsyth CBE*	65
Roasted Venison Haunch with Dauphinoise Potatoes and Braised Red Cabbage	*Chris Coubrough*	66

Meat

Harrington's Moroccan Barbequed Lamb	*Nigel Harrington*	67
Lamb Chops with Sauté Potatoes and Garlic with Asparagus	*Jonathon Holloway*	68
Peanut Butter or Groundnut Stew	*Thandi Kuzvinzwa*	70

Vegetarian

Sweet things

Desserts

Cakes and Biscuits

Inedible Delights

Soups, Snacks and Starters

Smoked Haddock Chowder

- 1lb diced potato – ¼ inch cubes
- 6oz onion, finely diced
- 6oz bacon, finely diced
- 4oz leek, finely diced and blanched
- 12oz smoked haddock, diced and chunky
- Milk and cream, ratio of 3 to 1

This is one of our most popular dishes and has always been a favourite with me. It can be served as a starter, light lunch, or as a more substantial meal served with a green salad. For such a tasty meal, it is surprisingly easy to prepare and serve.

Chris Hyde, Chef, Wroxham Barns

www.wroxhambarns.co.uk

Bring the milk, cream and potatoes to the boil, stirring well to prevent the ingredients catching.

Simmer until the potatoes are cooked and liquid is starting to thicken slightly.

Meanwhile sweat off the bacon and onion until cooked. Strain off excess fat.

Add the bacon and onion to the potatoes with the blanched leeks and smoked haddock. Simmer for 2-3 minutes, correct seasoning and serve with hot crusty bread.

"Anything you want it to be" Soup

- 1 kilo bacon bones
- 2 Spanish onions
- 1 green and one red capsicum
- 4 cups cooked kidney beans
- Lots of butter
- One beef stock cube or home-made stock

Chop onion, garlic and capsicum.

Melt butter in saucepan and cook garlic onion and capsicum until not quite soggy. Put in bacon bones and cooked kidney beans and cover with water.

Add one beef stock cube (or home-made beef stock if you have it and really like/want to impress your guests). Put lid on saucepan and simmer for 4 - 5 hours. Let stand overnight and serve the next day with fresh bread and lots of butter.

A significant part of my life was spent in a household that had 4 generations of women. There was my motorcycle riding, atheist grandmother who could sew like a demon and dressed us in matching home-made coats and hats. There was my manic depressive mother, who could dance up a storm and make a party if there was a beat and another person in the room. There was me, a 17 year old single mother and my one year old daughter, who was doted on for being the sunshine in our lives that she was. There were also two great aunts, one with a beard and the other, the only member of the family who had managed to hold down a 'regular' job.

Night after night, my grandmother would ask the same question..."What do you feel like for dinner love? I thought we might have chops and salad".

"That would be great Nan", I would answer as though it were a new thought every day. My mother would roll her eyes and comment how she'd had to put up with someone who couldn't cook all her life.

Years later, Nan had passed on and my mother had taken over as the matriarch. We would go to Mum's for a "home-cooked" meal that was either take-away pizza or the one and only soup that she knew how to cook but would call it by several different names in an attempt to fool us.

On special occasions, mum, despite not having 2 cents to rub together would get "Gra gra" otherwise known as Graham the Caterer to deliver a feast. Apparently Gra Gra was awarded numerous contracts for catering from the government department my mother held an administrative position in.

Now, all of my mothers and aunts have passed and I have been handed the mantle of matriarch. Unlike my forebears I love cooking. The first recipe I taught myself outlined above was perfected by going to a Hungarian restaurant on numerous nights during a two month period until I perfected their bacon bone and bean soup.

In acknowledgement and memory of my wonderful women who have passed I serve this up as "Anything you want it to be soup".

Leanne Minshull, Director of Strategy and Liaison, Senator Bob Brown, Australian Green Party

Asparagus Soup

- 3 large bunches Norfolk asparagus
- 4oz (110g) salted butter
- 1 large onion, peeled and thinly sliced
- 1 small potato, peeled and thinly sliced
- 2 pints (1.2 litres) white chicken or vegetable stock
- 6oz (175g) spinach leaves
- ¼ pint (150ml) double cream
- Salt and pepper to taste

Cut the asparagus tips off so they are about the length of your middle finger. Lightly peel the bottom 2.5cm towards the cut end to create a neat white stalk and a plump green top. Retain the peelings. Put the tips to one side as they can be used in other dishes, such as the Norfolk Asparagus with Rosti Potatoes, Streaky Bacon and Hollandaise. Chop the stalks and add to the peelings.

In a large pan, melt half the butter over a medium heat, then add the sliced onion and potato. In another saucepan heat the stock. Once the onions and potatoes are soft, add the asparagus stalks and trimmings, and pour in the hot stock. Bring to the boil and simmer until the stalks are tender.

Take off the heat, add the spinach and whizz up in a liquidiser or food processor. Finally push through a fine sieve: the easiest way to do this, I find, is with the back of a ladle.

Just before serving, bring the soup up to room temperature, add the remaining 2oz (55g) butter and the cream, and check the seasoning. Serve topped with some blanched, buttered asparagus tips and a thin strip of crispy streaky bacon.

You cannot beat local Norfolk Asparagus.

Galton Blackiston, Morston Hall

www.morstonhall.com

Butcher's Beetroot Soup

- 450g beetroot
- 15g butter
- 110g chopped onions
- Salt and freshly ground pepper
- 1 litre vegetable stock (or 850ml stock and 150ml creamy milk)

Chive Cream:

- 4-6 tablespoons sour cream or crème fraîche
- 1-2 tablespoons finely chopped chives

Wash the beetroot carefully under the cold tap. Don't scrub, just rub off any earth with your fingers. Don't damage the skin or cut the ends or it will bleed its colour during cooking. Put the beetroot into a pan, cover with water, bring to the boil. Then reduce the heat and simmer, covered, for anything from 20 minutes to 2 hours depending on their size and age. The beetroot are cooked when the skins rub off easily. When cool enough to handle, rub off the skins and chop the beetroot. Melt the butter in a heavy-bottomed saucepan over a medium-low heat. When it foams, add the onion. Season well, stir, then cover with a 'lid' made from baking parchment, putting the paper right on top of the onions. Cover the pan, turn the heat low and sweat over a gentle heat for 10 minutes. Meanwhile, bring the stock to the boil. Add the beetroot to the onions with the stock. Season, then purée with a stick blender or *carefully* liquidise in batches. Re-heat, adding more stock or milk if you like to get the consistency you like, and adjust the seasoning.

Serve garnished with swirls of sour cream and chopped chives.

After making this, you may well look like you've got blood on your hands...

Jon Baker, The Voice Project, Neutrinos and The Butcher of Common Sense

www.voiceproject.co.uk   www.neutrinos.co.uk

Cazuela de Lentejas y Chorizo –

Lentil and Spicy Sausage Pot

- 400g jar of lentils
- 2 litres water
- 30ml oil
- 1 medium tomato, chopped
- 1 medium onion, quartered
- 1 green pepper, chopped
- 1 bay leaf
- 1 head of garlic, separate the cloves
- 1 teaspoon salt
- 2 cloves
- 2 large potatoes, chopped
- $\frac{1}{4}$ teaspoon each of cumin, paprika and ground pepper
- Dash of cayenne
- 200g chorizo sausage, chopped

Serves 6

In a large pan add the first 10 ingredients. Bring to the boil then simmer slowly for one hour. Meanwhile, in a mortar, crush the cumin, paprika and pepper together with the cayenne. Add to the pot with the potatoes and the chorizo. Cook for a further 30 minutes until the potatoes are tender. Serve.

Potajes and Cazuelas are thick casserole-type soups, usually containing chickpeas and pulses. They are typically served as a first course but are substantial enough to be a main dish accompanied by bread.

The reason I think these are great is that they are really tasty and so simple!

Susan Coates, Constitution Motors

www.constitutionhyundai.co.uk

Dorothy's Apple Soup

A soup with a curious flavour that few people can identify – but far more often than not, they come back for more and demand to know the recipe. It also has the merit of a dish which uses up less than perfect fruit.

Serves 4-6

- 2lbs cooking apples, weighed *after* peeling, coring and removing any blemishes, bruising etc.
- 1 pint water
- A stock cube
- 1 dessertspoon sugar
- 3 teaspoons mild curry powder

Cook the apples in the water with the stock cube to a mush. Whirl in a blender. Add the sugar and curry powder. Re-heat and serve. If you find you prefer a sweeter, saltier and/or more spicy flavour, add more sugar, some salt and more curry powder.

This recipe came from a lady who ran her own top fruit orchard in Berkshire for many years. She also taught us how to store apples. Pick only sound fruit, avoiding bruises but don't worry too much about skin blemishes. Place six to eight large apples or double that number of small ones in a supermarket plastic bag and loosely tie the handles together. Store each bag on a flat surface in a cool, dark place (a loft with an insulated floor is ideal). The apples give off a gas (the appley smell) which confined to the bag acts as a natural preservative. Check each bag once a fortnight and remove any rots. Carefully handled this way most apples will stay sound well into the new year.

Roger Turff, King's Lynn

Fresh Leek Soup

- 2oz (50g) butter
- 1½ lb (675g) leeks, cleaned and finely chopped
- 1oz (25g) flour
- 1 pint (600ml) home made stock or 2 chicken stock cubes dissolved in 1 pint (600ml) water
- ½ pint (300ml) milk
- Salt and pepper to taste
- A little cream if desired

Melt the butter in a large saucepan.

Add the leeks and fry gently, stirring occasionally without browning for 5 minutes.

Stir in the flour and cook for 2 minutes.

Gradually add the stock, stirring continually.

Add the seasoning and milk.

Bring to the boil and simmer for 40 minutes.

Taste and check the seasoning.

At this stage a little cream may be added if desired.

Simple and delicious.

Jim Green, Able Community Care

Good Carrot Soup

- 1lb (450g) carrots
- 1 small onion
- 1oz (25g) butter
- 1½ (750ml) pints of chicken stock (or 1½ (750ml) pints of water and 2 chicken stock cubes)
- 3 strips of orange peel
- 1 bay leaf
- Salt and pepper to taste

Peel and slice the carrots and onion.

Melt the butter in a pan and add the vegetables.

Cover and cook gently for 5 to 10 minutes.

Pour on the stock or water and stock cubes.

Add the orange peel, bay leaf and seasoning. Bring to the boil.

Cover and simmer for about 15 minutes or until the carrots are tender.

Remove the bay leaf, sieve or liquidise the soup in a blender.

Taste and check the seasoning. If the soup is too thick, thin down with extra stock.

Re-heat and serve.

Croutons

Take day old white bread.

Cut into ½ to 1 inch strips, leaving the crusts on.

Cut the strips again to form cubes.

Deep fry until golden brown.

Remove from the pan with a slotted spoon.

Drain the croutons onto kitchen paper.

Allow ½ a slice per person.

Croutons freeze well, and if large amounts are made at the same time they can be stored and removed when required and warmed in the oven.

Myra Green, Able Community Care

Kevin's Roast Parsnip Soup

Serves 6-8

- 1 onion
- 2 cloves garlic
- 1 kg parsnips
- Herbs
- 2 tablespoons olive oil
- 3 tablespoons honey
- Seasoning
- 1½ litres chicken stock
- 450ml double cream

Roughly chop onion and garlic and place on a roasting tray with the peeled parsnips cut into chunks.

Season and sprinkle with herbs (sage, thyme, rosemary etc) and place into a heated oven (200°C) for 30 minutes until tender.

Place most of the chicken stock into a saucepan add the cream and bring to the boil then simmer.

Add the roasted vegetables and continue to simmer.

De-glaze the roasting pan with the remaining stock and add to the saucepan.

Allow to cool slightly then transfer to a blender and blend until smooth.

Return to pan to re-heat and season to taste.

Serve with vegetable crisps.

This is a simple yet delicious winter soup. I am a keen cook but like the simplicity of this recipe using one of my favourite vegetables. It is popular amongst friends and family – indeed it was the first thing requested by a relative after open heart surgery!!

Kevin Horne, Chief Executive
Norfolk and Waveney Enterprise Services (NWES)

www.nwes.org.uk

Lentil and Lemon Soup

- 1 large carrot, chopped very small or grated
- 1 large onion, chopped very small or grated
- 3 tablespoons oil
- 8oz split red lentils
- $1\frac{3}{4}$ pints water or very light vegetable stock
- 1 teaspoon ground turmeric
- $1\frac{1}{2}$ teaspoons whole cumin seeds
- 2 slices root ginger (size and thickness of 10p coin)
- 1 bay leaf
- 2 lemons
- Salt and freshly ground pepper
- Chopped coriander leaves to serve (optional)

Serves 4

Gently sweat the onion and the carrot in the oil for 5 minutes. Then add the cumin seeds. Stir and continue to sweat until the onion is transparent. Do not allow to brown.

Add the lentils, turmeric and ginger. Stir and cook for 2 minutes.

Add the water or stock and bay leaf and bring to the boil, reduce heat to a simmer and cook for 25-30 minutes until the lentils break up when well stirred.

Add salt and pepper to taste - do not add the salt before cooking the lentils as this toughens the skins and prevents them breaking up.

Remove the ginger and bay leaf.

Take two slices out of the middle of each lemon. Place a slice of lemon the bottom of each serving bowl, giving it a squeeze to release some of the juice. Pour the soup on top. Use the remaining ends of the lemons to squeeze juice over the surface of the soup - do not stir in - leave the juice making a trail in the soup, so you get the delicate flavour of the soup contrasting with the sharpness of the lemon.

Sprinkle chopped coriander on the top if you wish.

This is the first recipe I ever made up. I had something similar in an Indian restaurant. It was the first time I had ever taken someone out for a meal – for a friend's birthday, when I was in my teens. Despite the restaurant trying to overcharge me by falsifying the bill, I remembered the taste of the soup and tried to recreate it.
I have tweaked it since – in those days I couldn't buy ginger or leaf coriander – and have added more lemon.

Sarah Passmore, UEA graduate

Portugese Red Bean Soup

- 1 large onion finely chopped
- 2 decent sized chorizo sausage chopped into small pieces
- 1 litre chicken stock
- 2 small tins chopped tomatoes
- 2 small tins red beans
- 3 large potatoes (maris piper) cut into decent size chunks
- Olive oil

In a large pan, fry onion and chorizo in a small amount of olive oil.

Add chicken stock, tomatoes and beans plus juice.

Simmer for 2 hours. Add potatoes and cook until just firm.

Serve with bread.

This recipe brings back many happy memories of Bermuda. Portugese Red Bean Soup was brought to Bermuda from the Azores.

Barbara Cappoci. The Green Man Jazz Club, Norwich

Potaje a la Catalana –

Catalan Bean Pot

- 400g jar of garbanzos (chickpeas)
- 2 litres of water
- 1½ onions, chopped
- 1 bay leaf
- 50g lard
- 4 tomatoes, peeled and chopped
- 50g pine nuts
- 150g butifarra (white sausage) chopped
- Salt and pepper
- 2 hard boiled eggs, chopped

Serves 6

Heat the chickpeas with the half chopped onion and bay leaf in a pan with the water. Bring to the boil and simmer for 30 minutes. Melt the lard in a frying pan, sauté the whole chopped onion until soft. Add the tomatoes, pine nuts and sausage. Cook on a medium heat until reduced, about 15 minutes. Season with salt and pepper and place in an earthenware casserole.

Add the lentils and enough of the cooking liquid to make a thick soup. Cook for another 20 minutes and serve with the hard boiled eggs.

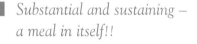

*Substantial and sustaining –
a meal in itself!!*

Fiona Coe, Phill Coe Photography

www.phillcoe.com

Cheese Straws

- 2oz butter
- $2\frac{1}{2}$ oz plain flour
- 3oz mature cheddar cheese
- Yolk of 1 egg
- $\frac{1}{4}$ teaspoon salt and a little pepper
- 1 tablespoon cold water if required

Grate cheese finely.

Mix with flour, salt and pepper.

Rub in butter.

Lightly whip yolk with half of the cold water.

Make a hole in the dry ingredients and pour in the egg mixture to form into a stiff dough.

Add more water if required and finish mixing with hands.

Roll out thinly (3/10th inch) and cut into strips about 4 inches long and 3/16th of an inch wide.

Put onto a greased baking tray and cook in a moderate oven 140-150°C for 8-10 minutes.

NB. The egg white can be used to make meringues.

These cheese straws are crunchy and melt in your mouth – nothing like the leathery shop-bought equivalent. But be warned: They are very more-ish!

Richard Cross, Abbey Farm Sandringham Estate

Cheese Pudding

(The Plain Man's Soufflé)

- 8oz (225g) fresh white bread, cubed
- 6oz (175g) grated cheese
- 3 eggs
- 1 pint of milk

Put cubed bread into a basin and add the cheese and the eggs.
Warm a pint of milk and pour into the mixture.
Mix it well. Add salt and a nice big grind of black pepper.
Transfer to a 2 pint dish and bake in a moderately hot oven, 190°C/375°F/Gas 5 for 50 minutes.
When you take it out it will be all puffed up and brown.
Serve with salad or baked beans.

I sometimes use a little more cheese and a little less bread. This cheese pudding is a quick and easy supper dish if someone calls in unexpectedly.

Barbara Allison, Able Community Care

Eugene's Beef Burger

- 1½ lbs of ground beef 25% to 30% fat content
- DO NOT USE LEAN BEEF!
- 6 whole spring onions finely chopped
- Handful of flat parsley rough chopped
- 1 large garlic clove crushed (optional)
- 1 large egg
- 2 tablespoons of oyster sauce
- 2 tablespoons tomato ketchup

Mix all the above ingredients thoroughly, leave in fridge for 1 hour. Then make six round balls and flatten into burger shapes. When putting on barbecue do not turn for several minutes, turn and repeat. This is to create a skin each side so as they do not fall apart.

The key to this recipe is to use fatty beef, NO SALT as this dries the burger, and careful handling on the barbecue.

This is the most fantastic burger recipe, for the "barby season" which really works for juicy burgers that are tender and tasty.

Eugene Charlier, The Catering Experience, Weston Longville
www.thecateringexperience.co.uk

The Original Egg Banjo

I am a terrible cook, but when I get very hungry I remember something that we used to eat at all hours, snatched between patrols in Belfast in the early 1970's – The Original Egg Banjo.

It is quite simple. Take two pieces of white bread and butter them on one side.

Fry two eggs, so that the yolk is still runny. Put the eggs between the bread, with salt and pepper to taste, as a sandwich.

Stand slightly back as you eat the banjo, to avoid the runny yolk and enjoy this wonderfully unhealthy instant meal.

General Sir Richard Dannatt, GCB, CBE, MC

Egg Mousse

- 6 hardboiled eggs
- 2 tablespoons anchovy essence
- 1 tablespoon tomato ketchup
- ½ packet Davis Gelatine
- 3 tablespoons water
- ½ pint mayonnaise
- Black pepper and salt
- A little cream
- Handful of prawns (optional)

Hard boil eggs.

Serves 6

Dissolve gelatine in the water.

Mix together chopped egg, anchovy, tomato ketchup, cream and prawns (if included) salt and pepper.

Add mayonnaise plus the dissolved gelatine.

Mix it all together, put in a bowl or ring.

If you use a ring you can fill the centre with chopped cucumber and prawns. Serve with toast and butter.

A very tasty starter!

**H.M. Lord-Lieutenant of Norfolk
Richard Jewson JP**

Chicken Mayonnaise

- One 4lb chicken cooked
- 1 tablespoon olive oil
- 1 small chopped onion
- 1 level tablespoon curry powder
- $\frac{1}{4}$ pint of stock (chicken or Swiss bouillon powder)
- 1 rounded teaspoon tomato purée
- Juice of half a lemon
- 2 rounded tablespoons of apricot jam
- Sweet chutney
- Half a pint of mayonnaise
- 3 tablespoons of single cream
- Button mushrooms

Heat oil in a saucepan, add onion and fry until soft.

Stir in curry powder and cook for a few minutes.

Add stock, tomato purée, lemon juice, apricot jam, chutney and sliced mushrooms.

Tip into a basin and let it cool.

Stir in mayonnaise and cream.

Add cooked, diced chicken.

Cover and put in the fridge. This tastes much better when it has had time to chill.

Wonderful with salad and fresh crunchy bread.

**Chris Goreham and Julie Reinger,
BBC Radio Norfolk, BBC Look East**

Feta finger
with cranberry, orange & mint dip

Serves 2

- 4 sheets of filo pastry
- 100g feta
- Melted butter
- 2 oranges
- 5 stalks of mint
- 1 tablespoons cranberry sauce

Butter one filo sheet. Place another on top and butter. Cut into 4.

Repeat for other sheets.

Cut feta into 8 sticks and place diagonally on segment of filo. Roll up tucking ends in.

Peel & segment oranges, squeezing all juice out. Roughly chop the mint leaves and add along with cranberry to the orange. Blitz with hand blender adding some orange juice.

Place fingers on a baking tray in a medium oven until lightly browned for around 10 minutes.

Serve with crisp fresh salad leaves.

A delicious light starter or snack.

**Emma Wilcox, Head Chef,
Pulse Café/Bar, Norwich**

www.pulsecafebar.co.uk

Welsh Rarebit

- 6oz dry, well-matured Cheddar or Leigh cheese
- 1½ oz butter;
- Good 2½ fl oz brown ale
- Salt; pepper; cayenne
- Squares of fresh hot toast (dry or buttered)

Grate the cheese. Melt the butter in a shallow saucepan or small sauté pan. Add the ale with the cheese and plenty of seasoning. Set the pan on a gentle heat and stir continuously until smooth and creamy, but do not get more than just hot, otherwise the mixture will be stringy. Turn at once on to the toast arranged in a hot dish and serve.

I really didn't know about Welsh Rarebit for many years or what the difference was between it and cheese on toast or toasted cheese, thinking they were all pretty well the same.... well they most certainly are not! The addition of the ale makes for a revolutionarily different dish. It's worth going out and buying a bottle of beer just to give it a try. It's most amazing how the taste of cheese is changed by the addition of a little alcohol.

Dave Holgate, Stonemason, Norwich

Fragrant Thai Prawn Omelette

- 5 really good quality eggs (for preference Cotswold Leg Bar from Clarence Court)
- 4oz good prawns or shrimps (I always buy shell-on prawns – more hassle but better flavour)
- 2 tablespoons fish sauce (Nam Pla) available in every supermarket and Asian food store
- A couple of finely chopped spring onions or a tablespoonful of chopped chives or wild garlic leaves
- 1 or 2 finely chopped bird's eye (or similar) small chillies
- As much chopped coriander leaf as you like – I like lots!
- A couple of tablespoons of water
- 1 tablespoon of toasted sesame oil

For 2 people as a light supper dish with some crusty bread and salad or as part of a Thai dinner for 4.

Crack the eggs into a bowl and beat the white and yolk together with a fork. Add the fish sauce and water and stir into the eggs. Heat the oil in an omelette pan or other non-stick frying pan or wok.

When fairly hot, add the eggs and keep them moving with a spatula or wooden spoon until they start to set. Remove from heat and cover with a close-fitting lid. When they have almost set, sprinkle all the remaining ingredients over the middle. reserving half of the coriander leaves for decoration.

Fold the edges of the omelette over the middle, put the lid back on and replace on a medium heat until completely set. Ease out of the pan, turning the omelette over if possible without breaking it up and place on a warmed dish. Sprinkle the remaining coriander over the top.

Now enjoy!!

Jude Orange,
Norwich Puppet Theatre

www.puppettheatre.co.uk

"No-Fail" Yorkshire Puddings

- 2 eggs
- 1 cup milk
- 1 cup flour
- $\frac{1}{2}$ teaspoon salt

Break eggs into a bowl.

Add milk, flour and salt.

Stir until just blended; the mixture is still slightly lumpy at this stage.

Pour into 8 well-greased muffin tins or individual Yorkshire Pudding tins.

Place in COLD oven!!

Turn heat to 450°F/Gas 7.

Bake 25 minutes without opening the oven.
Turn off heat.

Remove the puddings from the oven. Prick to let out the steam and return to cooling oven for 10 minutes.

Pack in plastic bags and freeze. When required simply re-heat for 5 minutes in a hot oven.

As a Yorkshire woman, I was sceptical when given this recipe by a Canadian friend, but it works every time and I have no qualms about passing it on.

Beryl Hadfield, Doncaster
Reader of Able Community Care Gazette

Sunflower & Sesame Seed Roast Potatoes

- 1lb (450g) potatoes
- About 4 tablespoons vegetable oil
- 2 medium onions
- Cracked pepper and sea salt
- A sprinkle of Bouillon powder (or stock cube)
- A good handful of sesame seeds
- A good handful of sunflower seeds

Peel if necessary and par-boil potatoes for 5 minutes.

Pre-heat oven 220°C/430°F/Gas 7 and prepare large roasting tin with oil.

Peel 2 medium onions and chop into rings.

Place roasting tin in oven until hot but not spitting.

Drain and leave to stand to cool and dry off. Give them a shake in the pan (keep the lid on!) to roughen them up a bit.

Tip potatoes carefully into roasting tin. The oil must be very hot in order for the potatoes not to stick to tin. Turn the potatoes carefully in oil and season with cracked pepper, sea salt and bouillon powder (or stock cube). Leave space between potatoes for best roasting results.

Place roasting tin in the oven on middle shelf for 15 minutes.

Remove and turn potatoes once more and re-season. Place onions on the potatoes and return to the oven for another 20-30 minutes until golden brown.

For the last 5 minutes add sesame seeds and sunflower seeds sprinkling liberally.

Serve with traditional roast or even salads.

My film credits include working with the Muppets and Jim Henson's Creature Shop, Walt Disney Films and with Director Tim Burton, on Charlie and the Chocolate Factory and Sweeney Todd - the Demon Barber of Fleet Street, a film in which I pop up briefly only to come to an untimely and grisly end. Watch closely and you will see Sweeney Todd (Jonny Depp) slit my throat in his barber's chair and send me down the shoot – only to be made into a meat pie! – No that's not my recipe, I'm a Vegan.

I travel a lot and spend long periods away from home so when I was asked about my favourite recipe many great meals went through my head from many parts of the world but hey, you know what? ...I always come back to a great roast. Yes, the old traditional roast! It's a real treat that reminds me I'm back and one meal that's best served at home. Being vegan too, what I love most is trying different twists on the theme. This recipe focuses on the potatoes.

Phill Woodfine
Film Co-ordinator / Animatronics
Performer and Puppeteer

Ekoori

- 3 tablespoons unsalted butter or vegetable oil
- 1 small onion, peeled and finely chopped
- ½ teaspoon peeled and very finely chopped ginger
- ½ -1 fresh hot green chilli, finely chopped
- 1 tablespoon very finely chopped green coriander
- ½ teaspoon ground turmeric
- ½ teaspoon ground cumin seeds
- 1 small tomato, peeled and chopped
- 6 large eggs, lightly beaten
- Salt and freshly ground pepper to taste

Melt the butter in a medium sized, preferably non-stick frying pan over medium heat.

Put in the onion and sauté until soft. Add the ginger, chilli, fresh green coriander, turmeric, cumin and tomato. Stir and cook for 3-4 minutes or until tomatoes are soft.

Put in the beaten eggs. Salt and pepper them lightly. Stir the eggs gently until they form soft, thick curds. Cook the scrambled eggs to your preferred consistency.

Serve with toast or any Indian Bread.

This recipe is donated in memory of my happy time working for Able Community Care.

Lord Cartner of Hales

Spitfire Sauce

Multiply the following quantities depending on how much sauce you are making:

- 10-30 chillies depending on type and size (ideally fresh)
- 1 green capsicum pepper
- 1 large onion
- 2 garlic cloves
- 1 teaspoon sugar
- 1 teaspoon salt
- 150ml vinegar

Roughly chop the peppers (removing the seeds will produce a better flavour to heat ratio), onions and garlic and heat in a pan with the other ingredients for 30 minutes. Blend in a food processor before pouring into warmed glass bottles and sealing. Once opened, keep the sauce in a refrigerator.

This is my version of a sauce I brought back from the West Indies when I was a young man. It is not for the faint-hearted but provides a sweet hot tang as an accompaniment to many savoury dishes. Chillies are easy to grow in abundance so this is also a useful way to store surplus fruits, and the bright orangey-red sauce in clear glass bottles make great presents.

You can try making it with a variety of different chillies and spices according to your taste. Using habenero chilli peppers, for example, will give you an extremely hot sauce, but even the more common long tapered peppers produce a wonderful colourful sauce to be taken in small doses!

By Piers Warren
Author of How to Store Your Garden Produce
(Green Books Ltd) and Principal of Wildeye –
The International School of Wildlife Filmmaking
(Norfolk, UK)

www.wildeye.co.uk

mains

Chicken Breasts in Cream & Pernod Sauce

To be served with broccoli and baby sweetcorns.

- 2 chicken breasts
- 4 spring onions
- 4oz cream
- 1 tablespoon Pernod
- 1oz butter
- Salt and freshly milled pepper

Heat butter in pan.

Add chopped spring onions and fry for 2/3 minutes over moderate heat.

Cut chicken breasts in half (flat-wise).

Add to pan and fry until cooked through (both sides).

Move onto a warmed plate.

Spoon approx. 4oz cream into hot pan and stir for 5/6 seconds, then add Pernod and stir.

Add salt and freshly milled black pepper.

Cook for 3 or 4 seconds more until all smooth and cooked through.

Arrange chicken breasts on serving plates and pour over the Pernod and cream sauce.

Dress platter with accompanying broccoli and baby sweetcorns and serve.

This is a favourite Bill devised some years ago and which he never tires of. He is always complimented when he serves this dish to friends and family.

Bill Treacher, Actor

Chicken Balti

- 1 onion
- 4 cloves of garlic
- 3 fresh tomatoes
- 1 red or yellow pepper
- Mushrooms (optional)
- 2 chicken breasts
- 1 teaspoon turmeric
- 1 teaspoon mustard seeds
- Tiny bit of grated fresh ginger
- Basmati rice
- Patak's Balti Paste

Fry onions in plenty of olive oil till golden with a teaspoon of turmeric and mustard seeds. Add ginger and garlic and fry for 2 minutes.

Cut up chicken breasts into chunks and add to frying pan. Keep flipping over chicken chunks till cooked on each side.

Add diced up pepper and cook in frying pan for 3 to 4 minutes. Add diced mushroom and fry for a further 2-3 minutes. Add chopped up fresh tomatoes (no need to skin) and fry till mushy for about 3 minutes.

Add three tablespoons of Balti paste to frying pan or more according to taste. Simmer and stir for approximately 10 minutes. Add a little water to moisten.

Make sure curry does not dry out - add more water if necessary. Soak rice in water $\frac{1}{2}$ hour before cooking. Then boil and simmer till cooked about 10 minutes. Serve with plain white yoghurt, poppadoms and mango chutney.

I like this recipe because it only takes about 40 minutes and it is tried and tested so I know it is a good one to use when inviting anyone over for a meal. It is of course very tasty. Using olive oil is less unhealthy than using the traditional ghee or butter. My friend Karin in West Cork always insists I cook this dish for her when I visit as she was so knocked out by it and how good it was. BJ also makes sure I cook this at least once a week as he also loves it.

Anna Lucas and BJ Cole

www.bjcole.co.uk

42

Chicken Curry

- 1 cooked chicken
- 1 clove of garlic
- 1oz curry powder
- $\frac{1}{2}$ oz sultanas
- 1 chopped onion
- 1 red or green pepper
- $\frac{1}{2}$ oz flour
- 2 chopped tomatoes
- 1 tablespoon tomato purée
- 1 pint chicken stock
- $\frac{1}{2}$ chopped apple

Serves 4

Dice the chicken and cook it in a pan with the chopped onion, pepper and garlic for 2 minutes.

Then mix in the flour, curry powder, tomato purée and cook for a further 2 minutes.

Slowly add in chicken stock, bring to the boil and add apple, tomatoes and sultanas.

When ready serve with brown rice.

This is very easy and nice to eat.

**Nigel Worthington,
Manager, Norwich Football Club 2000-2006**

43

Chicken Josephine

- 4 half chicken breast
- 60ml Malibu
- ¼ cup water
- 150ml pure cream
- 1 large or 2 small bananas (peeled and sliced)
- Pinch sugar
- ½ cup chicken stock
- 2 tablespoons plain flour
- Little butter & oil

Flour lightly beaten chicken breast and pan fry in a little butter and oil till cooked on both sides. Remove chicken, drain pan. Add banana and cook gently for 1 minute. Add Malibu, sugar and stock. Let gently reduce by a third. Add cream and place chicken back in pan and gently cook, allowing sauce to thicken. Serve chicken with sauce over top.

This is nice with a salad or steamed vegetables.

CHICKEN *Josephine was created by me after I was appointed head chef on an island resort at 22. My name is Jo but I thought that Josephine was a much stronger name. I was very proud of this dish and I received a lot of compliments from the customers. It was my signature dish on the menu and each new menu it still appeared.*

Jo Kydd, Chef, Fingal Bay, Australia

Chicken Matilda

- 2-4 chicken breasts as required
- 6 celery sticks
- 1 large onion
- 1-2 green or red peppers as required
- 1 tablespoon horseradish
- 1 tin chopped tomatoes
- Grated cheese

This is my mother's recipe but I do not know where it came from and have never seen it written down, so I have done my best. It is very good and easy.

Councillor Evelyn Collishaw, Lord Mayor of Norwich 2009-2010

Pre-heat oven to 200°C/Gas 4

Put chicken breasts in large baking dish with olive oil to prevent sticking and bake in oven for 30 minutes (until chicken is browned). Season with salt and pepper.

While the chicken is cooking, take a large frying pan and cook the chopped onion in some olive oil. Add the chopped celery and peppers in bite-size pieces and braise for 10 minutes. (Other vegetables could be added as available or to taste.) When the vegetables are cooked, add the tomatoes to the pan and a large tablespoon of horseradish sauce.

Take chicken out of the oven and add all the vegetable mix to the baking dish on top of the chicken. Grated cheese can then be added as a topping with some salt and pepper. Return dish to the oven for another 25 minutes. (Can be kept at a low heat if required and can also be re-heated.) Quantities can be increased or decreased as required.

Baked potatoes are very good with this dish to soak up the juices and these can be cooked in the oven at the same time. Rice can also be served with this dish.

Garlic and Herb Chicken

Serves 4

- 4 free range chicken breasts
- 1 packet of garlic and herb soft cheese
- 8 slices of Parma Ham
- Fresh basil leaves

Unfold the chicken breasts, using a knife if necessary, to create a pocket in the middle of each one.

Fill each pocket with a quarter of the cheese. Be careful not to overfill or the cheese will run out as it melts.

Wrap each chicken breast in Parma ham, creating a tight seal.

Place the chicken breasts on a greased baking tray and bake in the oven for 20-25 minutes at 180°C.

The Parma ham should be crispy, the chicken moist and succulent.

Chop fresh basil leaves over the top and serve with green beans and sautéed potatoes.

A delicious blend of flavours and textures.

David Whiteley and Amelia Reynolds, BBC Look East

Garlic and Lemon Chicken

- 1 plump free-range chicken
- 1 lemon
- 4-5 pieces cloves of garlic
- Sprigs of rosemary
- 1 piece of root ginger freshly grated
- Mixed herbs
- Olive oil
- Salt and pepper

Put half the lemon inside the chicken

Pierce breast, thighs and legs with a knife and fill the slits with pieces of garlic, rosemary and ginger.

Rub oil over the chicken, salt and pepper and sprinkle generously with herbs so that it's encrusted.

Add a few more drops of oil and juice of other half of lemon.

Then stick that too into the chicken with any left over garlic and ginger etc.

Roast in a medium oven for an hour or so.

This makes a very good Sunday lunch accompanied by whatever usual vegetables you like and it's great for picnics. Then you wrap it up in silver foil while hot, and especially on a Spring or Autumn day it's delicious because it'll still be warm.

It's been a great family favourite over the years.

Susannah York, Actress

47

Marinated chicken

with vegetables on a bed of fresh baby spinach

Cut up in chunks some tomatoes, aubergine, fennel and red onion. Toss in olive oil and put in a baking tray with a few cloves of unpeeled garlic, salt and pepper and herbs. Roast on high for 40 minutes. Turn occasionally.

Marinate 2 chicken breasts in olive oil and soya sauce for 20 minutes.

Then cook on a griddle pan - should take about 10 minutes.

Place a bed of raw baby spinach on a plate. Put the roasted vegetables on top.

Slice the chicken breasts widthways into about 5 pieces and place on top of vegetables.

 *Enjoy!*

Fiona Bruce, Broadcaster, BBC

Chicken breasts, skinned, either whole or cut into thin slices.

Pesto (either home-made or out of a good jar).

For the pesto mix together:

- $\frac{1}{2}$ clove garlic, chopped
- 3 handfuls of fresh basil leaves chopped very fine
- A handful of freshly grated parmesan
- Good olive oil

Very Quick Pesto Chicken

In a flat dish cover the chicken portions in pesto.

Leave them in the fridge all day if you can (but half an hour will do). When ready, bake them till they are done.

The cheese in the pesto makes a great crust (finish them off under the grill if you like).

Serve with salad or rice, or put finely sliced parboiled potatoes in the dish with them.

This is a good instant supper which seems cleverer than it is.

Libby Purves OBE

48

Summer Chicken Salad

- 1 packet of streaky bacon
- 2 chicken breasts
- 2 hard-boiled eggs
- 1 bunch of spring onions
- 1 packet of baby vine tomatoes
- 1 cucumber
- 1 packet of feta or blue cheese
- 1 cup of marinated black olives
- 1 bunch of fresh parsley
- 1 bunch of fresh coriander
- 2 baby cobb lettuce
- 1 avocado
- Fresh balsamic vinaigrette

Advance preparation: (As you prepare each item, add to one large salad bowl).

Roughly chop the hard-boiled eggs, spring onions and baby tomatoes. Skin and dice the cucumber. Cube the feta (or blue) cheese and add the olives, finely chopped parsley, and very roughly chopped coriander. Cover bowl with cling film or clean damp cloth.

Approximately one hour before serving: Follow cooking instructions for chicken and approximately 15 minutes before the end of cooking time, add the bacon. The chicken skin should be crispy and the bacon very crispy. Whilst chicken and bacon are in the oven, roughly slice the baby Cobb and add to salad mixture.

When the chicken has cooled slightly (but still warm), cut into chunks and add to salad with crumbled crispy bacon and sliced avocado. Toss entire salad – gently – with vinaigrette. Serve immediately – with garlic or herb bread if required.

Perfect for al-fresco dining!

The Rt Hon Sir John Major KG CH

Spice-Roasted Chicken with Mango Salsa

- 4 chicken Supremes
- 2 tablespoons olive oil
- 2 teaspoons ground cumin
- $\frac{1}{2}$ teaspoon ground turmeric

Mango Salsa:

- 1 mango, peeled and diced
- 4 tablespoons olive oil
- 1 small red onion, thinly sliced
- 1 tablespoon black mustard seeds
- $\frac{1}{4}$ teaspoon cumin seeds
- 1 tablespoon julienned fresh ginger
- 2 cloves garlic, thinly sliced
- 1 red chilli, seeds removed, finely sliced
- 2 tablespoons soy sauce
- Juice of 2 limes
- 2 tablespoons chopped mint or flat leaf parsley

Pre-heat the oven to 180°C

Chicken:

Combine the olive oil and spices and brush on both sides of the chicken. Season. Place in a roasting dish and roast for about 35 minutes or until the juices run clear. Cover tightly and rest for 5 minutes.

Mango Salsa:

Put the olive oil and onion in a saucepan and cook until the onion is tender and golden. Add the mustard seeds, cumin, ginger, garlic and chilli and cook gently until the garlic is just starting to colour. Remove from the heat and stir in the soy and lime juice. Season and cool. Stir in the mango and herbs just before serving.

To serve: Slice the chicken and arrange on the plate. Spoon over the mango salsa.

Suggested accompaniments are a green salad and new potatoes.

This is a delicious dish we sampled recently on a visit to New Zealand which has become a firm favourite on our menu.

Jean and John, Carrick's at Castle Farm, Swanton Morley

www.carricksatcastlefarm.co.uk

Alison's Pasta

- 2 cartons/packets of fresh cherry tomatoes
- Olive oil
- 300g of dried pasta shapes
- 2 cans of drained tuna
- 1 jar of basil pesto

Serves 4

Pre-heat your oven to 220°C/Gas 7. Place the cherry tomatoes on a baking tray. Cover with a generous glug of olive oil and mix together to coat the tomatoes. Bake in the oven for about 30 minutes until the tomatoes are squishy and have burst their skins.

While the tomatoes are roasting, cook the pasta in boiling water. Then drain it and return to the saucepan. Finally tip the tuna and cooked tomatoes into the pan with as much pesto as you desire. Heat through the ingredients, stirring frequently.

Serve with crusty bread, salad and your favourite wine.

This recipe just happened by accident really. Our cupboard was looking pretty bare and I made a meal from the ingredients I could find. The flavours work well together. It's so simple and very tasty.

Alison Schofield, Art Angels Greetings Cards, Norwich

www.art-angels.co.uk

Baked Salmon in Filo Parcels

Serves 4

- 4 fillets Scottish salmon
- 100g thinly sliced gruyère cheese
- 1 bag young leaf spinach
- 1 egg yolk
- 8 sheets filo pastry
- 4 sprigs fresh dill
- Seasoning

Lightly cook the washed spinach with a knob of butter.

Slice the salmon fillets in half lengthways (horizontally), and lay the gruyère cheese across the bottom halves.

Finely chop the cooked spinach and spread over the cheese. Then sprinkle with chopped dill and season.

Place the upper half of the fillets on top, forming four salmon "sandwiches".

Wrap a sheet of filo pastry around each fillet, sealing with a dab of water. Repeat with a second sheet of pastry so each fillet is wrapped in 2 layers.

Place in the middle shelf of oven at 180°C and cook for 16 minutes.

Take out of the oven and brush the parcels with egg yolk. Cook another 4 minutes.

Serve immediately with hollandaise sauce and vegetables.

I have to admit this is my husband's recipe – he's the better cook in our house!!!

Susie Fowler-Watt, BBC Look East

Char-Grilled Fish
with Summer Salsa Salad

Serves 4

- 2 large ripe but firm avocados, peeled and cut into small chunks
- 2 small garlic cloves, finely chopped
- 2 ripe but firm mangoes, peeled and cut into small pieces
- 2 large red finger chillies (depending on required taste)
- 6oz peeled cooked tiger prawns each cut into large chunks (use more prawns if a starter and not serving with fish)
- 3 spring onions, chopped
- Juice of 2 limes (or to taste)
- Pinch of salt and lots of coriander sprigs to garnish

Cut the chilli in half and scrape out the seeds. Cut into thin slices. Then simply mix all the other salad ingredients in together. (Caution in amount and strength of chilli is recommended!)

4 fish fillets of your choice (any sort that can be char grilled – eg: snapper, sea bass, salmon, bream, cod etc)

Brush fillets on both sides with olive oil and grill for 3-4 minutes at one stage skin side up (ensure skin is crisp).

Serve the fish with the salad.

What I love about this recipe, which originated and was adapted from my favourite fish chef of all time (Mr Rick Stein), is the freshness of ingredients and the simplicity and speed of a really delicious flavoured summer salad that is filling, tasty and incredibly good for you! The other great thing is that you literally throw absolutely everything in together (other than the fish!) and you can prepare the salad earlier.

Deb Jordan, Pensthorpe Wildlife Trust, Fakenham

www.pensthorpe.co.uk

53

Coda di Rospo Alla Livornese or

Monkfish with Peas
in Fresh Tomato Sauce

(Although there seems to be some suggestion the original recipe was for dogfish!!)

Serves 4

- 800g boneless monkfish
- 450g fresh peas
- 315g ripe tomatoes, peeled and chopped
- 20g flat leaf parsley
- 2 cloves garlic, peeled
- 6 tablespoons extra virgin olive oil
- Salt and poivre noir

Cook peas till tender

Chop half of the parsley and garlic

Sauté for 1 minute

Add teaspoon of salt and cook 1 more minute

Add the tomatoes and cook on medium heat for about 20 minutes to give a concentrated sauce with very little liquid.

Cut fish into 2 inch chunks and add to the reduction.

Cook for 5 minutes, add peas and lots of black pepper.

Cook for a further 5 minutes and adjust seasoning as necessary.

Coarse chop the rest of the parsley and strew before serving. (Pardon the phrase!)

Bon Appettito (I think)

This is a delicious rather unusual dish for special occasions.

Wine suggestion – Ovieto Classico Secco

**Rt Hon The Viscountess Knollys OBE DL
Vice-Lord-Lieutenant of Norfolk**

Enjoy Some Tasty
Freshwater Crayfish

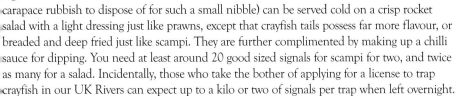

Signal crayfish when boiled in water for five minutes, (they turn a lovely 'lobster- red') and the succulent tail segment removed from the shell (I know there is a lot of carapace rubbish to dispose of for such a small nibble) can be served cold on a crisp rocket salad with a light dressing just like prawns, except that crayfish tails possess far more flavour, or breaded and deep fried just like scampi. They are further complimented by making up a chilli sauce for dipping. You need at least around 20 good sized signals for scampi for two, and twice as many for a salad. Incidentally, those who take the bother of applying for a license to trap crayfish in our UK Rivers can expect up to a kilo or two of signals per trap when left overnight.

Once boiled, hold each crayfish in both hands, with your thumbnails touching, and gently 'twist' to separate head and carapace from the tail end. Then, using a pair of scissors, snip through the underside casing of the tail and separate meat from shell. This leaves the tail with a 'dodgy-looking' dark, end that obviously cannot be eaten. Simply pull it backwards towards the narrow end (with the red side facing upwards) and its alimentary canal should come out all in one piece.

Rinse each tail under the tap and put into a bowl before popping into the fridge, whilst deciding on how to eat them. For those who do not go fishing simply purchase a tub of crayfish tails from the local supermarket and follow my recipe. You can of course quickly make up a tangy sauce from mayonnaise, tomato sauce (or purée) lemon or lime juice, plus black pepper and a little salt, and mix them into an elegant, giant glass along with chopped tomato, lettuce and red onion, as a sort of 'de-luxe crayfish cocktail'. There's nothing like impressing your friends. Or, and I do admit to this being my favourite, you can knock up a 'Tempura Batter' and fry your crayfish tails (just like those starters you get in 'Thai' restaurants) along with some vegetables like button mushrooms, slithers of carrot or florets of broccoli etc. I've even used florets of elder flower when in season, and it's all scrumptious.

Make up a tempura batter by beating an egg yolk with 8fl oz. ounces of 'iced water' (most important this) and then sieve-in 4oz of plain white flour. Mix together well and don't worry that the resulting batter appears 'lumpy'. Heat your vegetable oil to around 180 degrees in a wok (two inches deep should do) and after dipping each tail in the batter and shaking off any excess, lower in 'a few at a time', cooking each for just 2-3 minutes. Afterwards, drain on paper napkins and keep warm till eaten. Lastly, make up a plum/chilli sauce of your choice for dipping. All that work of separating tails from shells will have seemed worth it after all. Fry the vegetables exactly the same way in the same batter, and do not overcook. *ENJOY!*

One of my favourite dishes and one that I can collect the ingredients for while I'm actually fishing.

John Wilson MBE, Kazan River Productions

Fricassée of Smoked Haddock

- ¾ lb un-dyed smoked haddock
- 2 leeks
- 2 tablespoons frozen peas
- 2 medium tomatoes
- 2 tablespoons single cream

First skin the smoked haddock and cut into large chunks.

Clean the leeks. Cut them in half lengthwise and chop finely. Slice tomatoes.

In a frying pan put some butter and vegetable oil.

Cook the leeks until soft. Lay peas and sliced tomatoes on top.

Then put on the smoked haddock pieces. Pour the cream over it all.

Now cover it all with a lid or some foil and cook until the fish is done (about 10 minutes). Serve with small boiled potatoes. Nothing else is needed.

This is a dish I like very much as it's so simple, and apart from the touch of cream is sustaining without being rich.

It is the "Actor's friend".

PS It also allows you to quaff lots of white wine!!

Peter Bowles, Actor

Paella Paradise

- Onion: Large Spanish, finely chopped.
- Garlic: A few cloves, sliced.
- Red pepper: One, sliced into strips.
- Petit pois: One cup.
- Red chillies: Two, halved, de-seeded and sliced.
- Tomatoes: Three, chopped.
- Seafood: 12 uncooked king or jumbo prawns, shelled; squid (400g), sliced.
- Chorizo: Half a sausage, roughly chopped into cubes.
- Chicken thighs, skinned and boned: Four, halved into large pieces.
- Paella or risotto rice: One cup.
- Sherry: A generous splash.
- Saffron: One teaspoon.
- Thyme: A few small sprigs.
- Olive oil: 2 tablespoons of extra-virgin.
- Boiling water: Just enough to cover all ingredients.

Serves 4-6

Heat olive oil in a large, deep frying pan (moderate heat).
Add chorizo and stir fry for 10 seconds.
Add onions and continue to stir fry for 30 seconds.
Add chillies, red pepper, garlic, thyme and continue to stir fry for 2 minutes.
Add chicken and continue to stir fry until chicken is sealed.
Add sherry and fry for another 30 seconds to evaporate alcohol.
Add the rice and gently mix until it has become well coloured.

Pour the boiling water in.
Sprinkle the saffron in.
Add the seafood.
Add the tomatoes.
Add the petit pois and gently mix all the ingredients through once.Simmer gently for about 10 minutes.
Serve and enjoy!

This recipe has evolved continually since my student days and we eat it regularly. I LOVE Chorizo and practically lived on the stuff when I was travelling!! Traditionally rabbit is used in this dish but chicken is just as good.

Matthew Brewin, Able Community Care

Prawn Spag

- Linguine - 1 pack for 4
- Olive oil
- Finely chopped medium onion
- 3-4 cloves garlic - finely chopped
- Half big red chilli finely chopped
- 6 anchovy fillets chopped (from a tin)
- 2 packs raw king prawns (if raw not available cooked are ok - but just pop in at end to warm through - not cook!)
- Parsley - good bunch - finely chopped
- Parmesan - finely ground

Heat a good slug of oil in pan (30mls - not too much but it's good for you!) Add onion, garlic, chilli. Fry gently - do not brown.

After about 5 minutes - add anchovies and mash in with wooden spoon. (They 'disappear') On low heat continue to cook 20 minutes or more. (This can all be done in advance and let cool - the ingredients impregnate for added taste).

Boil pasta to 'al dente'.

Just prior to above put prawns cut in half into sauce to cook - maybe only 1 minute if raw - to keep soft.

Add pasta to the sauce - stir and mix.

Sprinkle a little parmesan in for taste - mix and then add handful of parsley and mix.

Serve with extra parsley and parmesan on top of pile of pasta for decoration and taste. Can also be made with strips of smoked salmon added in at the end instead of the prawns.

My wife says I am out of practice cooking - but I have managed this recently. A friend of mine cooked it for me and I asked for the recipe. I love seafood and it reminds me of sunny holidays!

Bon appetit!

Norman Lamb MP for North Norfolk

Salmon Fillet with Parmesan Crust

- 1 salmon fillet per person
- Grated cheddar cheese and some Parmesan cheese, enough to top each fillet
- Large pinch herb "Provence" or fresh herbs and/or parsley

This recipe is delicious, quick, easy and healthy: A good dish for the end of a busy day at Hope and Homes for Children as it takes very little time to prepare!

Cook skin side of fish first for about 5 minutes in the oven.

Turn over fish and put cheese and herbs on top.

Press down on each fillet.

Place under the grill for 3-5 minutes until brown and crispy.

Check the salmon is cooked through.

Serve with new potatoes and peas or broccoli.

Colonel Mark Cook OBE, Hope and Homes for Children

www.hopeandhomes.org

Trout with Almonds

- 2 fresh trout, cleaned
- 2 handfuls of almonds
- Butter
- Mushrooms
- Peas

This was the first meal I cooked for my husband-to-be over 40 years ago!!

Prunella Scales CBE

Slash the trout three or four times on each side and fry in butter until well browned on each side.

Cook the peas, drain and dress with butter.

Slice and fry the mushrooms in butter until tender.

Brown the almonds in a lightly buttered pan and serve together with the fish, peas and mushrooms on heated plates.

Shrimp/Prawn Gumbo

- 2lbs (1 kilo) shrimp/prawns
- 3 tablespoons oil
- 2 tablespoons plain flour
- 3 cups okra, chopped
- 2 onions, chopped
- 1 tin tomatoes
- 2 pints water
- 1 bay leaf
- 1 teaspoon salt
- 3 cloves garlic
- Chilli pepper (optional)

First peel and de-vein the raw shrimps/prawns or defrost raw tiger prawns.

Next make a dark roux using the flour and half the oil. Do this by heating the oil in a heavy pan and gradually adding the flour stirring constantly. Cook over a low heat, always stirring, until the roux is the colour of pecan shells. This will take about 25 minutes.

Add the shrimp or prawns to this and stir for two minutes then remove from the heat and set aside.

Now smother the onions and okra in the remaining oil and fry until the okra is nearly cooked.

Add water, bay leaf, garlic, salt and pepper. Add shrimp or prawn and roux mixture to this. Cover and cook slowly for 30 minutes. Serve in soup bowls with rice.

Gumbo is a South Louisiana creation. The name "gumbo" comes from the Congo word for okra, "quingombo." It can be made with okra or with file as a thickening agent. File is the powdered sassafras leaf made long ago by the Choctaw Indians.
My recipe uses okra as it's more readily obtainable.

Nicola Banham,
Chilsong Korean Martial Arts, Norfolk

www.chilsong.com

Swordfish Mexicali

- 4 Swordfish steaks

- 1 teaspoon of coriander flakes
- ½ teaspoon of chilli flakes
- 2 tablespoons of lime juice
- 150g butter
- Salt and Pepper

Soften the butter, add all the dry ingredients, mix well then add the lime juice.

Make into a log shape and wrap in cling film and refrigerate until needed.

Pan-fry the swordfish steaks 3-4 minutes and turn over and cook for a further 2-3 minutes.

When cooked slice off 2 rounds of the butter and put on top of each steak and melt in the oven or under a grill.

Serve with fine green beans and sauté potatoes with a wedge of lime.

Delicious and simple to execute.

**Joan Armstrong, Head Chef
Grandano's Restaurant, The Mustard Pot,
Whinburgh**

www.mustardpotmexican.co.uk

Zarzuella

- 3 thick slices of sourdough, chopped up
- 12 large almonds, skinned and toasted
- 2 cloves of garlic, finely chopped
- 1 large onion, finely chopped
- 1 small chilli (optional)
- 2 bay leaves
- 2 tins chopped tomatoes, drained
- 2 tablespoon of tomato purée
- 1.5 litre fish stock or a very light chicken stock
- 1 large glass of white wine
- 2 tablespoons of sherry (fino if you have it)
- 2 small lemons
- 1 bunch of flat leaf parsley, roughly chopped
- Salt
- Olive oil
- 400g of chorizo, finely sliced or diced
- 600g of firm fleshed white fish such as monkfish, bass or pollock cut into 1-2 inch pieces
- 600g of shellfish, I like to use a mixture of cockles, clams and mussels but one will do.
- 600g of squid, the baby frozen stuff is good for this. They come with the beak and ink sac removed, so take out the feather (looks like a piece of plastic), cut the head in half and lightly score the inside in a criss-cross pattern. The tentacles can go in as they are.
- 600g of prawns, (again I use head-off frozen tiger prawns for this and peel them leaving just the tail). The squid and prawns can be quickly defrosted by placing in a bowl of cold water.

Begin by frying the bread in some olive oil until golden, then whizz in a food processor along with the almonds whilst drizzling in some olive oil until a loose paste is formed, set aside.

Clean the shellfish by sitting in running water for 10 minutes, to remove any grit. De-beard the mussels if you are using them and discard any that don't close. Shake the shellfish. Boil the wine and add the shellfish, put a lid on and steam until they are open, discard any that don't open and set aside.

In a very large pan (everything is going in) fry the onions, garlic and chorizo on a low heat until the onions have softened and the oils are running from the chorizo. At this point you can add a little chilli if you like it spicy! Add the tomatoes, tomato purée and bay leaves and heat through.

In a hot pan brown your fish, squid and prawns quickly (they will cook in the big pot), de-glaze the pan with the sherry and add to the cooking pot.

Add all of your fish and shellfish cover with your stock (you may not need it all). Season to taste with salt and simmer for 10 minutes. Gently stir in the bread and almond paste you made earlier along with the chopped parsley and the juice of the lemons.

Serve in a bowl with some nice bread.

This is a Catalonian recipe and reminds me of holidays in Spain, a nice thought coming out of a English winter! I like to use chorizo in mine for the paprika flavour.

Iestyn Thomas, Chef, Norfolk

Congham Pigeon Breasts in Red Wine

Serves 4

- 8 pigeon breasts
- Olive oil
- Red wine
- Butter for frying
- Chopped onion
- Stock
- Bay leaf

Beforehand:

Marinade pigeon in olive oil and red wine.

Pan-fry pigeon breasts in butter until cooked but still pink – keep warm.

Use pan for frying chopped onion. Add red wine and reduce by half.

Add stock, pepper and bay leaf and reduce to taste.

Pour over pigeon breasts and serve.

If you haven't tried pigeon before, do give this recipe a go!

Henry Bellingham MP for North West Norfolk

Pheasant with Lime and Ginger

- Pheasant breasts
- Whole limes
- Fresh ginger
- Garlic

Heat oil in a pan until hot and seal the meat.

Remove to a plate and add to pan the garlic, juice of 4 limes and sliced fresh ginger.

Cook over a low heat until soft and add a little stock and grate the rind of the limes into the mix. Then replace the pheasant and cook for 5 minutes over a low heat.

Put in a warming oven to rest and then serve with fresh lime slices and grated peel.

An alternative to traditional roast pheasant.
The limes and ginger give this dish a delicious twist.

Sir Nicholas and Lady Bacon, Raveningham Hall

www.raveningham.com

Kentish Hot Rabbit Casserole

As a boy in the fields of Kent in the Second World War I recall that our almost only meat source was taken right from the countryside. With all that rationing, Londoners were wan and pasty but the country folk were encouraged to help the war effort by reducing the wild wood pigeons and rabbits ... which we did with gusto, and stayed fit on pigeon pie and rabbit casserole.

The rabbit is fat-free, all lean meat, and highly nutritious. Disadvantages? It pongs during the skinning, paunching and quartering, but never during cooking or eating. So the wise counsel is to find a good poulterer/game merchant and buy an oven-ready wild rabbit. (Do not be coddled into buying a hutch-raised "tame" job – they are as bland as white bread).

Two other disadvantages: wild rabbit is naturally dry and can be tough. After all, the meadow rabbit is extremely fit and runs like hell. Being fat-free it needs moisturising and tenderising in the cooking. Hence my recommendation: long, slow casseroling in a tasty sauce.

So ... disjoint your rabbit to achieve five portions; forelegs, muscular rear legs and saddle (lower back). There is nothing on the ribcage area.

Slice a large Spanish onion and lay the discs at the base of the casserole dish. Anoint copiously with olive oil.

Place the five joints on top. Dust meat with two teaspoons of powdered hot mustard.

Complete the filling of the dish with knobs of swede, turnip, parsnip or all three, plus thick discs of raw potato and knobs of carrot.

Top up to the brim with your sauce; water-based but well anointed with rough wed wine, cheap port or (as in the war when we didn't have these), strong cider. A bumper of cheap brandy can also make life interesting.

A glazed earthenware crock works, or one of those heavy iron casseroles. Replace the lid and give it an hour in the top of the Aga, overnight in the lower oven and a quick fifteen minutes back in the top before eating. It should need no added "bits" and the meat should fall off the bone.

Then retire for a nap by the fire.

One rabbit does two people or a single very hearty eater.

All the solids come from our countryside and it's how we won the war in Kent.

Frederick Forsyth CBE

Roasted Venison Haunch with
Dauphinoise Potatoes and Braised Red Cabbage

Braised Red Cabbage

- 1 red cabbage
- 2 bay leaves
- $\frac{1}{2}$ cinnamon stick
- $\frac{1}{2}$ cup brown sugar
- $\frac{1}{2}$ cup redcurrant jelly
- 1 cup orange juice
- 1 cup red wine
- $\frac{1}{2}$ cup orange marmalade
- Pinch ground mixed spice
- 3 star anise
- Salt and pepper

Trim out the different muscles from a haunch of venison. You are looking for 200g pieces.

Season and oil the venison. Seal in a hot pan and place straight into a hot oven at 200°C for 12 minutes.

Remove venison from oven and rest for 3 minutes on a board in a warm place.

Carve into about $\frac{1}{2}$ cm slices and place on Dauphinoise potatoes with braised red cabbage and sautéed foraged mushrooms.

Spoon a venison jus around the outside.

Dauphinoise Potato

- 3 large potatoes, peeled and finely sliced
- 500ml cream
- 2 tablespoons grated parmesan
- 1 sprig thyme
- 1 clove garlic

Shred the cabbage and put into a large pan.

Add all other ingredients and cover with tin foil.

Cook in the oven for 2-3 hours, Gas 4.

Crush the garlic into a paste. Heat the cream with the thyme, garlic and seasoning. Line the bottom of the tray with greaseproof paper and cover with a layer of potato. Pour over a little cream and some parmesan. Continue with alternate layers of potato and cream. Finish with cream and parmesan on top. Bake in oven 180°C to 20-25 minutes until golden brown and potato is cooked.

The perfect combination of tastes, textures and colour.

Chris Coubrough, The Flying Kiwi Inns, Norfolk

www.flyingkiwiinns.co.uk

Harrington's Moroccan Barbequed Lamb

- Half leg of lamb
- Zest and juice of half a lemon
- 3 cloves garlic crushed
- Heaped teaspoon ground coriander
- Heaped teaspoon ground cumin
- 1 teaspoon Ras al Hanout
- 1 teaspoon paprika
- Cayenne to taste
- Pepper
- Salt

Butterfly the lamb, mix everything else together and rub into the meat. Leave overnight and barbecue the next day.

Start meat off on grill setting furthest from coals, turn frequently and close barbeque lid if you have one. Leave to rest before slicing and serving with pitta bread, salads, tabbouleh and a mint and yoghurt dressing.

We lived in Norwich for 10 years, and most years had a barbeque with friends on Nigel's birthday in mid July. This was one of the most successful and simple recipes, and became an annual favourite. Whenever we do this dish now it brings back memories of scorching Julys in our garden in the black rectangle (that's north of the golden triangle). Now living in Northern Ireland, the focus in mid July is rather different … wetter too!

Susan Mason and Nigel Harrington, Belfast

Lamb Chops, Sauté Potatoes and Garlic with Asparagus

Four or eight small organic lamb chops, depending how hungry you are.

- Madeira or Marsala, a small glassful
- Some double cream
- Some potatoes, nutty ones, diced to be a bit smaller than garlic cloves
- Twenty cloves of garlic, peeled
- Truffle salt, if you have it, otherwise sea salt
- A large bunch of fresh Norfolk asparagus, whole trimmed spears
- Alioli, if you have it
- Sea salt and pepper
- Olive oil, for cooking

First, part boil the potatoes in salted boiling water for ten minutes, then add the garlic cloves and continue for another ten minutes, until they are all soft. Drain them, breaking them up a tad in the process.

In your favourite large heavy frying pan, heat some olive oil. Throw in the potatoes and garlic cloves on a fairly high heat, add a good couple of pinches of truffle salt (or sea salt) as you like, and sauté them until crispy and brown (the garlic cloves will end up brown on the outside and gooey on the inside).

Meanwhile, heat a griddle as hot as possible with the smallest amount of olive oil. Seal both sides of the lamb chops, then turn them so that the fat is facing down and either battle to make them balance or hold them all together with one of those wooden food tongs. The key is pink meat and crispy skin. Oh, and tomorrow you really should go to the gym.

When the meat is cooked and the potatoes are done, put the potatoes/garlic in a bowl and the chops onto the four warm plates. Now do two things at once: with the left hand put the asparagus spears in the potato frying pan, cook fast and turn until browned on two sides, sprinkled with a little salt. With the right hand, pour the Marsala or Madeira

into the still hot lamb griddle, then at the last minute add a splash of cream.

Serve the asparagus onto the plates next to the meat, and throw the potatoes back in the pan to re-crisp, then put them on the plates, pour the creamy sauce over the meat, put a dollop of alioli on the asparagus and leave the potatoes and the garlic cloves dry.

Eat. Enjoy. Feel guilty or don't. If no alioli, don't worry, probably better for you.
To be healthier, skip the cream.
To be even healthier, eat a salad.

This is my favourite indulgent "girls in bed at 8.30pm and I want proper grown-up food by 9.30pm" meal.

One of the best things about my job is that I get to travel to Festivals, sometimes in beautiful places, and always try and buy a small jar of something - hence the truffle salt (from Tetsuya in Sydney) and the alioli (garlic mayonnaise made with just garlic and oil, eaten in Catalunya many times but now bought in a great place near Liverpool Street)! I'm also prone to interchanging ingredients.

Jonathon Holloway
Director of the Norfolk and Norwich Festival

www.nnfestival.org.uk

Peanut Butter or Groundnut Stew

- 1 kg boneless lean beef (tender cut)
- 3 shallots
- 1 clove garlic (can add more its optional)
- 1 green pepper
- 1 red pepper
- 1 medium red onion
- 3 tablespoons peanut butter
- $\frac{1}{4}$ tin chopped tomatoes
- Squeeze of lemon juice
- $1\frac{1}{2}$ litres beef stock
- Olive oil
- Salt and pepper

Cut beef into medium size cubes.

Chop all vegetables into small pieces.

With a thick based large sauce pan shallow fry the meat in olive oil till crisp and golden brown.

Add to the meat all the vegetables except the tomatoes.

Fry everything together till golden brown.

Blend together peanut butter and tomatoes with half of the beef stock.

Pour mixture into the meat and vegetables.

Pour the rest of the stock into the pot.

Add salt and pepper and lemon.

Cover the pot and on slow heat let it simmer for 1 hour

Pour blend into meat and vegetables in the saucepan and stir till it starts simmering.

Lower heat and cover the saucepan and let it simmer for about an hour stirring from time to time.

Serve with rice, polenta or potatoes.

Tender and Tasty.

Thandi Kuzvinzwa, Able Community Care

Linguine con le fave e pancetta

(Linguine with broad beans and pancetta)

- Olive oil
- 2 cloves of garlic peeled and chopped
- 1 red onion peeled and chopped
- 150g pancetta sliced and chopped
- 200g broad beans

- ½ kg linguine
- Handful of grated parmesan
- A good slug of white wine
- Salt & pepper
- Flat leaf parsley, washed and sprigged

Serves 4

Heat olive oil in a frying pan and throw in all ingredients from the first section, stir and allow onions and garlic to soften and broad beans to gently cook. Cook linguine in a pan of salted boiling water until al dente. While the pasta is cooking check that the broad beans are tender, adding a good slug of white wine so the sauce is moist but not liquid. Drain the pasta adding a little of the pasta water to the broad bean mixture. Finally gently combine the linguine with the sauce throwing in a handful of parmesan and seasoning. Serve immediately garnished with parsley.

I first grew broad beans a few years ago on our small vegetable patch and wanted to use them in a dish that highlighted rather than drowned their subtle flavour - there is nothing better than releasing the freshly picked beans from their silky pods, though if you can't find fresh, frozen beans can work well. In Italy we often eat young tender broad beans raw with thinly sliced pancetta and freshly baked bread or as a soup with peas and mint. Buon appetito!

Raffaele and Gail Tevola,
The Olive Tree Restaurant, Ellingham

www.olive-tree-restaurant.co.uk

71

Durango

This is a recipe from West Africa - in English it's spelled "Durango", but the "ngo" at the end is really more of a Portuguese nasal sound, "o" pronounced through your nose, which expresses the delightful texture of the dish well.

This is the luxury version - if you're strapped for cash, leave out the meat. Vegetarians can substitute a starchy vegetable for the meat (not one that contributes much of its own moisture, though). Remember that the rice is the food, and this is the sauce.

- Good oil, about 6 tablespoons. Traditionally, palm oil or ground nut oil. (Yes, this is not a low-fat dish.)
- 1 medium to large onion.
- ½ kilo of medium-diced lamb or beef. Especially good are filleted neck of lamb or skirt of beef.
- Between 3 and 6 red chillies, complete with innards. Or 1 Scotch Bonnet pepper for the strong.
- 1 can of good quality chopped tomatoes in juice.
- 2 teaspoons of sugar.
- 150g or more of smooth peanut butter - the kind with palm oil.
  (For this version, I've added 200g button mushrooms. This would cause bewildered amusement in Senegal.)

Chop the onions finely and sweat them, covered, in the oil until they are soft. Roughly chop the chillies and add them in, stirring well for a few moments. Add the meat and fry until it has lost its red tint. This is not an English stew, so don't overheat at this stage. Add the illicit mushrooms if you must. Let it bubble, stirring, until the mushrooms have started to shrink. Then add the tomatoes and sugar and bring to the boil. Boil for a minute or two, stirring, and then add the coup de grace - peanut butter, into the pan, and stir until it's the texture of hot lava - little craters should emerge round the bubbles as they erupt.

Cover and simmer for hours (at least 2) stirring quite frequently. Without the stirring it will curdle, and the deep russet palm oil will rise to the surface. Every Mandinka mother knows that this is not acceptable, and will delegate a daughter or two to stir the pot constantly to prevent it, being careful to scrape the sauce that collects on the sides of the pot back into the mixture, and periodically add a little water to maintain the texture just right. Here in the lazy North we don't know any better, and don't tend to have spare daughters standing around, so just be sure to stir the oil back in thoroughly, like mixing an old can of paint, till it's all merged in again.

Cook enough rice for everybody and unexpected guests, wash your biggest enamel basin or gather round the bath, tip the rice into it, turn out the durango on top, wash your hands, and enjoy!

Alternatively, this can be served onto plates, I suppose.

David Glendining
Director, Keisaku Design
& Development Ltd.

www.keisaku.co.uk

73

Norfolk Braised Beef in Beer with Herb Dumplings

Serves 6

Braised Beef:

- 1kg Norfolk braising beef (try Salamanca Farm, Stoke Holy Cross)
- 1 or 2 onions – sliced
- 200g dark-gilled mushrooms – sliced
- 2 or 3 celery sticks – sliced
- 3 large peeled carrots – cubed
- 2 tablespoons oil
- $\frac{1}{2}$ teaspoon dried or 1 teaspoon fresh thyme
- 1 pint best Norfolk Ale
- 1 tablespoon plain flour
- Salt
- Ground black pepper
- 1 tablespoon Worcestershire sauce*
- 1 tablespoon soy sauce*
- 1 tablespoon tomato puree*

(*optional as not from Norfolk!)

Herb Dumplings:

- 200g self-raising flour
- 100g beef or vegetable suet
- $\frac{1}{2}$ teaspoon salt
- 2 tablespoon chopped mixed herbs (parsley +thyme +sage +rosemary)

Braised Beef:

Dice beef and coat in flour and seasoning

Heat oil in frying pan and brown meat in 4 batches – quick and hot!

Same with onions and celery (you may need a bit more oil).

Put meat, all vegetables, flavourings, herbs and seasonings into large ovenproof casserole.

Pour beer into frying pan and bring to boil to dissolve the brown flavourings from the pan. Add this to the casserole.

Heat oven to 140°C (130° fan oven) /Gas 2-3 and cook for 2 hours until the meat is tender and delicious.

Dumplings:

(sometimes called '20 minute swimmers')

In a mixing bowl combine flour, salt and suet. Add approx 125ml cold water to make a dough, soft but not sticky.

Divide dough into 12 and roll in floured hands.

For the final 20 minutes of casserole cooking time, put dumplings on surface of stew and replace the lid.

Serve with lightly cooked green vegetables and some Colman's mustard mash.

Enjoy with a glass of beer brewed in Norfolk

Jake Humphrey, BBC Sport

Pork Chops with Cream and Mushrooms

- 6 large pork chops (trimmed of excess fat)
- 50g butter
- 2 teaspoons chopped fresh or 1 level teaspoon dried thyme
- 350g mushrooms
- Juice of 1 large lemon
- 1½ tablespoons plain flour
- 150ml double cream
- Salt and freshly milled black pepper

Serves 6

Pre-heat the oven to 180°C/350°F/Gas 4

Place a large double sheet of cooking foil on a meat roasting tin. (Please bear in mind that it must be large enough to wrap the chops in.)

In a frying pan brown the chops on both sides in butter then transfer them to the foil. Season each one with salt, pepper and a little thyme.

Roughly chop the mushrooms (I like to use a mixture of mushrooms but all button works just as well) and fry them in the same pan adding a little more butter if needed. Then pour in the lemon juice letting it bubble for a minute and then add the flour and stir in until the mixture is soggy. (Don't worry if it looks horrid at the stage – it always does!)

Spoon the mixture over the chops, some on each, then spoon a little cream over each one. Wrap up loosely with the foil, sealing securely, and bake for 1 hour. Serve the chops with the juices poured over.

This recipe is very rich and best served with rice and salad. Enjoy!

I particularly enjoy cooking this recipe as it needs little attention so I can get on with other things while it's cooking.

Rt Hon Charles Clarke

Slow Cook Shoulder of Lamb with Boulangère Potatoes

- 1 whole shoulder of lamb
- 1 head of garlic, peeled and separated into cloves
- 2 medium onions
- 4 large potatoes, peeled
- 1 bunch of thyme, picked
- 1 pint of chicken stock
- Salt and pepper

Slice the onion on a mandolin very thin. Then slice the potatoes lengthwise on the mandolin.

In a baking tray or oven proof dish that is about 8cm deep and will fit the lamb shoulder, put a layer of onions, then thyme leaves and season.

Then add a layer of potatoes overlapping each other to completely cover the onions.

Then do another layer of onions and thyme leaves.

Then do another layer of potatoes.

Repeat the process until you have none left.

With a small knife, make inserts into the lamb shoulder and fill the holes with whole garlic cloves.

Pour the chicken stock over the top of the potatoes to just cover.

Place the lamb on top of the potatoes.

Season and put in the oven at 130/140°C for 4 hours.

Remove and cool slightly.

The lamb should be golden and the potatoes crispy on the top and moist underneath. The lamb should flake away from the bone with a fork.

Serve.

This is very easy to cook and full of flavour with wonderful aromas.

Tom Kerridge, The Hand and Flowers, Marlow

www.thehandandflowers.co.uk

Spicy Paprika Pork

- 4 pork chops cut into strips or 1lb diced pork

Marinade:

- 2 tablespoons olive oil
- 1 tablespoon paprika
- 1 chopped onion
- 2 cloves garlic
- 1 teaspoon ground ginger
- $\frac{1}{4}$ teaspoon cinnamon

Serves 4-5

Marinate pork for at least $\frac{1}{2}$ hour.
Fry off then add:

- 1 tin chopped tomatoes
- 1 tablespoon tomato paste
- 1 tablespoon cider vinegar
- 100gm chopped dried apricots

Simmer for $\frac{1}{2}$ hour then add a tin of chickpeas.

Garnish with chopped parsley and serve with rice or cous cous and vegetables if desired.

You could use chicken instead of pork.

This is a good meal for a crowd of people as it can be made the day before. If you double the quantity you only need to add the one tin of chickpeas – unless you happen to be a great lover of chickpeas!

Lettie Harris, Able Community Care

"Wok around the Clock" or
Stir Fry Beef with Ginger

- ½ pound of beef (sirloin, rump or fillet)
- Green peppers
- Bunch of scallions (spring onions)
- Globe of fresh ginger root
- Medium sherry
- Packet of cornstarch
- Extra virgin olive oil
- Salt
- Sugar
- Basmati rice

Cut beef into half inch cubes.

Mix in a cup of 3 tablespoons sherry with 2 tablespoons olive oil and 1 tablespoon cornstarch and a pinch of salt.

Pour mixture over beef to marinate for a few hours, stirring occasionally.

Chop peppers into small slivers.

Chop scallions into tiny rings.

Cut ginger root and cross-cut to tiny pieces.

Put rice on to boil for 12-15 minutes in saucepan.

Heat 2 tablespoons of oil in wok, add beef and stir-fry vigorously until meat browns, then remove to its dish again.

Clean wok, heat 2 further tablespoons of oil then add first chopped ginger root, then scallions. Stir-fry vigorously adding salt to taste.

Add green peppers to the mix and stir-fry thoroughly with chopped ginger and scallions.

Toss teaspoon of sugar onto peppers if required.

Add marinated beef again into these vegetables and stir-fry the whole even more vigorously.

Remove the mixture to a lidded tureen – same with rice to separate tureen.

Serve mixture onto a bed of rice and enjoy subtle blend of contrasting tastes.

I do not cook this dish often. But when I do it is a kind of a "family treat" and I love it so much myself that I often make enough to eat morning, noon and night – a kind of "wok around the clock" routine!!

It has no real connection with my 2 years as a hostage in China, except my dear late wife Shirley bought me a wok as a birthday present a few years after my return home with an American-published Chinese recipe book that called cornflour "cornstarch" and spring onions "scallions". She thought it might be nice to master proper Chinese cooking after my unpleasant culinary experiences in China, and this stir-fry dish became my "Plat de Resistance".

I love the great flourish of cooking in a wok quickly after long painstaking cutting-up preparations. The beef can of course be replaced with free range chicken to make another similarly delicious dish – and red/yellow peppers can be added to give enhanced colour to the dish.

If you are not a great cornflour fan, that ingredient can be dispensed with from the marinade.

I trust 'dear reader' you will enjoy this too.

So… Wok on… Wok on.. with hope in your heart and you'll never Wok alone! You'll never Wok alone!

Anthony Grey OBE

Sausage Meat Pasta

(Salsiccia a pezzi di pasta)

- 1 kilo sausage meat (any good quality sausage meat will do, but see note below)
- 1 heaped teaspoon of fennel seeds crushed in a pestle and mortar
- 125 ml glass of red wine (keep some of the rest of the bottle for the cook!)
- 75 ml Pastis (Pernod/Ricard etc)
- 1 tablespoon of olive oil
- 1 heaped tablespoon tomato purée
- Enough dried pasta for 4 (any type will do whatever you have in the store cupboard!)
- Salt/pepper to taste
- Parmesan cheese (Freshly grated)

Skin the sausages and slowly brown the meat in a shallow frying pan for 10-15 minutes, keeping it moving. (Good quality sausage meat should not give off too much fat or moisture, but pour off any excess if needed.)

Add the olive oil continue to cook.

Add the fennel seeds, red wine and Pastis a little at a time. As the liquid evaporates all the flavours will concentrate. Cook slowly for 5-10 minutes.

You are aiming for quite a dryish mixture.

Stir in the tomato purée, and cook slowly for a further 5 minutes. Boil and drain the pasta and toss in the mixture with another drizzle of olive oil, serve with the parmesan cheese sprinkled over.

This is a special recipe for me, as it was the first meal my wife and I had whilst among the packing cases on the first day when we moved into our new home in Norwich. It is so simple and easy to cook. I adapted it from watching an expatriate Italian/Norfolk friend of mine cook it for me.

Pickering's Sausage stall on Norwich Market does the most divine Sicilian mountain sausages which are meaty and full of garlic and just perfect for this recipe. Just skin them.

Apart from the pastis these are all simple store cupboard ingredients.

Damian Conway, Dipple and Conway, Norwich

www.dippleandconway.co.uk

Marrow Provençale

- 1 medium marrow, peeled
- 1oz butter
- 1 medium onion, finely chopped
- 1 clove garlic, crushed
- 1 green pepper, seeded and chopped
- 8oz tomatoes, chopped
- 4oz Lancashire or Cheddar cheese, grated

Cut marrow into 1 inch rings.

Remove seeds and cut rings into 1 inch cubes.

Melt butter in a large saucepan and fry marrow until golden.

Transfer to a plate.

Fry onion, garlic and pepper until golden.

Add tomatoes and marrow and mix well.

Place half the mixture into an ovenproof dish.

Sprinkle with 2oz of the cheese.

Add remaining marrow mix.

Sprinkle with remaining cheese.

Bake 190°C/Gas 5 for 30 minutes.

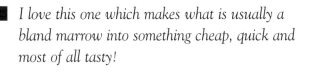

I love this one which makes what is usually a bland marrow into something cheap, quick and most of all tasty!

Wally Webb, BBC Radio Norfolk

millet and Vegetable Gratinée

- 4oz (100g) millet
- 1 pint (600ml) water
- 3oz (75g) butter or margarine
- 2 medium-sized leeks
- 1 large carrot
- 4 celery sticks
- 1oz (25g) 100% wholemeal flour
- 1 pint (600ml) milk
- 3 tablespoons chopped parsley
- 1 teaspoon sage
- ½ grated rind and juice of lemon
- Salt and pepper to taste
- 4oz (100g) cheddar cheese

The contrasting flavours and textures of millet and vegetables provide a satisfying savoury dish.

Cook the millet in the measured boiling water until just tender and all the water has been absorbed. Slice the leeks, grate the carrot and finely slice the celery. Melt 2oz (50g) butter in a saucepan, add the vegetables and sauté for 10-15 minutes, stirring frequently. Add the millet and stir over very gentle heat to keep warm. Meanwhile melt the remaining butter in a saucepan. Stir in the flour and cook for 1 minute. Stir in the milk, herbs, lemon rind and juice and bring to the boil. Reduce heat and simmer for 2 minutes. Pour it over the vegetables and stir well. Adjust seasoning with salt and pepper. Transfer to a warmed serving dish, sprinkle with cheese and "bubble" under a hot grill until golden brown.

This recipe is from my 1st cookbook given to me by Mum and Dad in 1985, from "Cranks" recipe book. The millet is unusual but cheap. The hint of lemon is delicious and it's easy to make in advance. Enjoy!

Helen McDermott, Radio and TV Presenter

Vegetarian Tart

- 1 packet puff pastry
- 2 red peppers
- 1 red onion
- 3 cloves of garlic
- 1 courgette/zucchini
- 8 cherry tomatoes
- 1 pot fresh pesto
- 1 ball good quality mozzarella
- 3 tablespoons olive oil
- Salt and pepper

Pre-heat oven to 200°C/Gas 6.

Chop vegetables into 3 cm pieces.

Place in large roasting tin and drizzle with olive oil.

Place in pre-heated oven and roast for approximately 45 minutes until tender.

Roll out puff pastry to size of baking tray.

Score 1cm border around edge.

Smear a thin layer of pesto onto the puff pastry.

Place roasted vegetables onto pastry.

Finish with torn mozzarella.

Season to taste.

Place back in oven for approximately 20 minutes until pastry is golden.

Serve with fresh green salad and crusty bread.

This is my daughter Kate's recipe – so it must be good!!

**Professor John Last, Principal
Norwich University College of the Arts**

www.nuca.ac.uk

The Aubergine Bake

- 1 large aubergine thinly sliced
- 2 teaspoons (10ml) olive oil
- 1 onion, chopped
- 1 clove garlic, crushed
- 4oz (125g) mushrooms, sliced
- 1 green pepper, deseeded and sliced
- 2oz (50g) unsalted cashew nuts, roughly chopped if large
- 1oz (25g) wholemeal breadcrumbs
- 1 tablespoon (15ml) tomato purée
- 2 teaspoons (10ml) chopped fresh basil
- 1 tablespoon (15ml) shoyu
- $\frac{1}{4}$ pint (150ml) water
- 1oz (25g) wholemeal flour
- $\frac{1}{2}$ pint (300ml) skimmed milk
- 1 egg
- 2oz (50g) Cheddar cheese, grated
- Salt and black pepper
- 2 teaspoons (10ml) grated parmesan cheese

Put the aubergine slices onto a large baking tray which has been lightly brushed with $\frac{1}{2}$ teaspoon of the oil. Brush the tops of the aubergine slices with another $\frac{1}{2}$ teaspoon of oil. Bake in a pre-heated oven at, 190°C/375°F/Gas 5 for 10 minutes then remove from the oven.

Heat the remaining oil in a large frying pan and gently fry the onion and garlic for 4-5 minutes. Add the mushrooms and pepper, cover and cook gently for a further 10 minutes.

Stir in the cashew nuts, breadcrumbs, tomato purée, basil, shoyu and sufficient water to make a moist mixture. Check the seasoning. You can use soy sauce in place of the shoyu but the flavour is not so strong.

Put about half the onion and nut mixture into the base of a large casserole or ovenproof dish. Top with half of the aubergine slices. Then put in the remaining onion mixture and cover with the rest of the aubergine slices.

Mix the flour, milk and egg in a blender or food processor until smooth. Alternatively, put the flour into a large bowl, beat the egg with the milk then gradually beat into the flour.

Put the milk mixture into a small pan and slowly bring to the boil, stirring continuously. Simmer for 3-4 minutes until thickened, stirring continuously. Remove from the heat and stir in the cheese. Check the seasoning.

Pour the cheese sauce over the aubergine mixture. Sprinkle with Parmesan cheese. Cover the dish.

Bake in the oven for 35-40 minutes, uncovered for the last 10 minutes and garnish with tomato segments. I usually serve it with a side salad.

I am surprised that the Aubergine Bake has captured the imagination of so many readers. But let me set the record straight on one or two points. The way Neil goes on about it you'd think I serve this meal up every week, but we don't have it anywhere near as often as he would have you believe! Besides, there's no way I could get Brats Major and Minor to eat it regularly.

In fact, I don't know of a dish called "Aubergine Bake". This recipe is Cashew Nut Moussaka!!

Mr and Mrs Neil Haverson, Fortress H

Guiliermo's Tomato Tart

- 500g of flavourful cherry tomatoes
- One tablespoon olive oil
- One tablespoon balsamic vinegar
- One teaspoon of chopped thyme
- One teaspoon of honey or brown sugar
- Salt & pepper
- Two red onions, finely sliced
- One package of chilled puff pastry
- 250g of crumbled goat's cheese
- Optional-handful of rocket or some fresh basil to sprinkle on top

Chop the cherry tomatoes into halves, add the olive oil and put into a heavy frying pan on a medium high heat.

When the tomatoes begin to soften (two to three minutes) add the balsamic vinegar, chopped thyme and honey or brown sugar to caramelize. Lower the heat and cover. Cook gently for a further ten to fifteen minutes. Add salt and pepper to taste. Meanwhile sauté the onions.

You may want to add a bit more olive oil or balsamic vinegar but you don't want the mixture to become too liquid. If the tomatoes have lots of juice or you add too much oil or vinegar you can always take the tomatoes out of the pan and reduce just the liquid. Don't overcook the tomatoes, you don't want them to dissolve into a mush.

Prepare the pastry as follows: Lay a square of puff pastry on a baking tray (approx. 30 cm square). Follow the instructions on the package for oven temperature etc. I make a raised edge around the parameter of the pastry by folding the pastry up and pinching it between my thumb and first finger. I also prick the surface of the pastry here and there with a fork.

Brown the pastry slightly in the oven before adding the filling. This keeps the base from going soggy. Watch the pastry carefully because it begins to rise quite quickly. When this happens don't be frightened! Just flatten the centre with a spatula and put it back into the oven. I do this several times until it begins to brown.

I think ceramic baking beads could hold the centre flat but they might keep it from browning, so I'm not sure if they would work.

Now spread the tomato mixture evenly over the pastry arranging the onions on top. Crumble the goat's cheese over the top and cook for ten to fifteen minutes. Remove from the oven. The tart will look and smell lovely.

Not all goat's cheese is particularly crumbly. Don't worry, just do your best.

Decorate with rocket. I like to toss the rocket lightly in vinaigrette first but you don't have to do this. You could also scatter some fresh basil on the top.

It's a colourful and flavourful dish that is relaxed and quick to make.

You could prepare the ingredients in advance and serve the tart as a tasty starter or as a main course with salad.

■ ■ ■ *This recipe was shown to me by a wonderful Argentinean musician, a singer and guitarist, who now lives in the UK. He made it in my kitchen as a contribution to the evening meal for a group of hungry musicians who had come to my home for dinner and to celebrate the arrival in London of the remarkable US jazz vocalist, Sheila Jordan.*

Ms. Chris Legee, Organiser of Singers' Night (established in 1996 in London) and UK agent of Sheila Jordan.

www.singersnight.co.uk

Lynsey De Paul's Tower of Veg

- Peppers x 6
  (*prep and cooking time: 35 minutes*)

Baked vegetable tower of mushroom, red and yellow peppers, wilted spinach, sweet potato, red onion confit and aubergine topped with grilled goat's cheese garnished with roast cherry tomatoes and a coulis of red and yellow peppers.

When making the tower make sure that your vegetables are large enough to fit properly in the cooking circle otherwise if they are too small they will not build up into a good tower.

Cut 3 red peppers and 3 yellow in half and place on baking tray.

Leave 5 red peppers whole for the coulis.

Salt them, drizzle olive oil and grid black pepper liberally.

Place in middle of oven at 225°C for 25 minutes.

- Mushrooms x 4
  (*prep and cooking time: 25 minutes*)

Peel 4 large Portobello flat mushrooms.

Put ground nut oil in frying pan and add a knob of butter – cook till golden brown.

Put salt on underside of mushroom and place in frying pan – add pepper.

Turn over and repeat the process. This only par-cooks them, but seals them first to retain flavour.

Place in oven for 10-15 minutes (together with peppers already there).

Put more ground nut oil in same pan – add knob of butter until melted only.

Throw spinach in a pan. Add salt/pepper and spinach and cook until wilted, stirring repeatedly.

Remember to take mushrooms out of the oven after 10-15 minutes. Take out the peppers, cut in half and leave the whole ones to continue cooking. Place half peppers on a tray to cool before peeling.

- Spinach – 4 packets
  (*Cooking time 5-6 minutes*)

Peel the sweet potatoes.

Slice thickly from the middle to get the largest circle

Put in microwave oven for 3 minutes on high to soften.

Season.

Put in pan with ground nut oil only. Cook until fork goes through.

Put on a plate with paper on it to soak off excess oil.

Take the peppers out of the oven.

- Sweet Potato x 2
  (*Prep and cooking time 10 minutes*)

Cut across the vegetable in 4 circles about $\frac{1}{4}$ - $\frac{1}{2}$ inch thick. (Try to buy large aubergines the size of the metal tube used for building the tower).

Clean fry pan by now.

Put olive oil on both sides of the aubergine before putting in the pan (They are like sponges and soak it up.)

Season with salt and pepper and cook until soft.

Put on a plate with paper on it to soak off excess oil.

- Aubergine x 2
  (*Prep and cooking time: 10 minutes*)

Continued over....

- Red Onion Confit
  (Prep and cooking time: 15 minutes)

Chop 6 small red onions into little pieces.

Put ground nut oil in a pan and a knob of butter.

Season with salt and pepper and cook until golden brown.

Add red wine or balsamic vinegar until brown colour.

Add 4 tablespoons of white sugar.

Put in a dish to cool and soak off excess oil.

- Pepper Coulis
  (Prep and blending time: 15 minutes)

Skin the whole red and yellow peppers.

Place in a blender.

Add salt and pepper to taste and blend. (If it is too thick to pour, add a little milk in the blender and blend again.)

Put coulis in a container with a spout so that it can be drizzled around the plate when serving.

(Prep and final cooking time of tower to plate: 30 minutes)

Building the tower – Place in a cylindrical metal cooking ring.

Peel the skins off the cooked peppers.

Place in the cooking ring starting from bottom up:
Mushroom
Red Pepper
Spinach
Sweet potato
Red onion confit
Yellow pepper
Aubergine

Put in oven on baking tray greased with oil and butter for 10 minutes to cook and "bed down" in the cooking ring. Place some small cherry tomatoes on baking dish at same time for garnish. Remove and top with goats cheese. Place under the grill until soft with a slightly browned top – 3 minutes. Remove baking tray from oven. Place tower still in ring in middle of dinner plate. Remove each cooking ring to expose tower of vegetables. Place two cherry tomatoes on the top of each tower. Garnish around it with red and yellow pepper coulis and caramelised vinegar.

I cooked this recipe on 'Celebrity Come Dine With Me'. It's one of my favourites.

Lynsey de Paul, Actress, Singer and Songwriter

Savoury Mediterranean Slice

Scone Mix:

- 450g self raising flour
- 100g butter
- 2 eggs
- Salt and pepper
- Small amount milk

Mediterranean Filling:

- ½ bag (110g) fresh spinach
- 125g mushrooms, sliced
- 1 onion, finely chopped
- 1 clove garlic, finely chopped
- 6 pieces sunblush, sundried tomatoes, chopped
- 2 tablespoons olive oil
- 150g pine nuts
- 150g chopped mixed nuts
- Seasoning

Serves 8 as a main course

Pre-heat oven to 200°C (180° for fan-assisted oven)/Gas 6.

Measure the flour, salt and pepper into a large bowl.

Add butter and rub into the flour until the mixture resembles fine breadcrumbs.

Break the eggs into a measuring jug, add milk and whisk.

Add to the flour mixture, mixing to form a soft dough.

Roll the dough out on to a lightly floured work surface to an oblong to fit into a roasting tin.

Top with the Mediterranean filling.

Bake in oven covered with foil for 10 minutes then uncovered for a further 10 minutes until well risen.

Serve with a side salad.

(This recipe will also serve 25 people as a snack. It is very fiddly to cut a large scone base into individual portions so make as individual small round patties of scone mix and vegetable mix combined together and then bake for 20 minutes).

This is a delicious and colourful recipe, ideal for Summer entertaining.

Newmarket House Clinic, Norwich

www.newmarket-house.co.uk

Poppy Seed Quorn Stir Fry and Cook Up

- 4 tablespoons olive oil
- 1 large packet quorn pieces
- 1 small chopped onion
- 3 cloves chopped garlic
- $\frac{1}{2}$ green pepper
- $\frac{1}{2}$ red pepper
- 1 tablespoon tomato purée
- 6-8 mushrooms
- Mange tout
- Fresh coriander
- Soy sauce
- Black pepper

Serves 4

In a large frying pan heat and the oil and add quorn pieces, chopped onion and garlic and fry till golden brown. Slice peppers and mushrooms and add and fry briefly. Season with black pepper and soy sauce and a sprinkle of Poppy Seeds. Add tomato purée and a cup of water. Stir well and cook on medium heat for 15 minutes. Add a handful of mange tout and some fresh coriander (Add another $\frac{1}{2}$ cup water) and stir for last 3 minutes. Serve with either white basmati rice or noodles.

Cook and eat with love.

Angela Harvey, Singer and Poet

www.poppyseedmusic.com

93

Sweet things

The Six Minute Syrup Sponge

- 2 Eggs
- Flour
- Butter/margarine
- Sugar
- Syrup

Weigh the two eggs. Each ingredient should weigh the same as the 2 eggs (eg: if the two eggs weigh 130g, then the butter, sugar and flour should weigh 130g)

Mix together.

Put about $\frac{1}{2}$ - $\frac{3}{4}$ of an inch of syrup in the bottom of a pyrex measuring jug.

Put the cake mixture on top.

Cover with cling film, making a pleat at the top to allow for the sponge to rise.

Put in the microwave for 6 minutes on high.

Test with a knife. The sponge might need an extra 30 seconds or so.

Serve with ice cream or custard.

I use this recipe all the time at home and when I was away caring on Jersey.

The sponge is very versatile. I have used apple purée and cooked blackberries, jam and chocolate. (Not all at the same time obviously!). All are absolutely delicious.

Alina Stammers,
Able Community Care Gazette Reader

A Different Bread and Butter Pudding

- 2oz (50g) butter
- 10 slices from a large loaf of white bread
- 10oz (275g) sultanas
- 2 bananas sliced
- 6 eggs
- 6oz (175g) sugar
- 6 tablespoons rum
- 2 pints (1.15 litres) milk

Grease a large, not too deep, ovenproof dish. Butter the slices of bread and layer them with the sultanas and bananas. Beat the eggs, sugar, rum and milk together and pour over the bread, then chill for 1 hour so that the mixture becomes really moist.

Bake in a moderate oven (180°C/350°F/Gas 4) for 45 to 60 minutes. Serve hot for a really sustaining pudding.

It's different!!

Sir Michael Caine

Apple Custard

- 1lb cooking apples
- 1 clove (or to your taste)
- 1oz margarine
- 2 eggs
- 3 tablespoons brown sugar

Serves 4

Peel, core and slice the apples, stew with clove(s) and very little water. (Too much water and the apples go soggy.)

When soft, remove clove(s) and allow the apples to cool slightly.

Then beat to a pulp and add margarine and brown sugar.

Beat the eggs and stir them into the apple mixture.

Pour custard into a greased oven dish (4 individual or one large dish) and place dish onto a baking tray.

Cook for 15 minutes on Gas 5 then reduce the heat to Gas 3 and then cook for another 15 minutes.

Serve hot or cold.

You can sprinkle a little grated dark chocolate on top if desired and add other ingredients before baking eg: rum essence, dates, raisins etc. I prefer it natural!

Very easy and comforting to eat!!

Aunt Leonora,
Able Community Care Gazette Reader

Apple Pancake Supreme

Prepare a pancake batter and set aside.

Wash the blackberries and simmer with golden syrup until soft.

Strain, reserving the juice and keep the fruit warm.

Return juice to the heat and bring to the boil.

Cream the cornflour in a little milk, pour it into the boiling blackberry juice, stirring all the time and cook until the juice thickens. Set aside.

Peel, core and chop the apples into chunks. Heat them rapidly with a little butter until they start to crumble at the edges, then remove from the heat and keep warm.

Next pre-heat a grill and a frying pan. Oil the pan. Once it is smoking, pour in all the pancake batter. As the bottom sets, but while the top is still liquid, take the pan off the heat, rapidly spoon in the apple chunks, blackberry blobs and strips of sauce. Swirl slightly so that the liquid batter blends a little but does not mix or cover completely. Sprinkle sugar generously over the top, then lemon juice and put under the red hot grill.

Serve immediately the top has caramelized.

This goes well with yoghurt or cream.

Ooops – sorry! I forget that not everyone cooks like I do – by eye!!

Bob Flowerdew, Organic Gardener, Norfolk

www.bobflowerdew.co.uk

Atholl Brose Cream

- 250ml double cream
- 1 tablespoon clear honey
- 1 tablespoon liqueur whisky (Drambuie works very well!!)
- Freshly squeezed juice of 1 lemon
- Small quantity of oatmeal

Serves 4

Combine ingredients and beat/whisk (quite easy and can be done by hand) until mixture thickens.

Spoon into small dishes or ramekins and put to chill in the fridge.

Before serving, sprinkle with lightly toasted oatmeal.

(This works equally well with half and half double cream and Greek-style yoghurt. You can also substitute brandy for whisky, make over a sponge or biscuit base and/or add fresh fruit when serving.)

I used to drink Prince Charlie's liqueur back in the day, so was overjoyed to find you could also eat the stuff (though probably not too much of it!). Countless cautionary clichés spring to mind, but do remember that oatmeal is supposed to be a cholesterol-buster!

Sally Hautot, Elsing

Baked Chocolate Mousse

- 9oz (250g) dark chocolate (minimum 70% cocoa solids)
- 12 fl oz (350ml) double cream
- 1 vanilla pod or 2 teaspoons vanilla extract (not essence)
- 6 fl oz (150ml) milk
- 3 medium or 4 small egg yolks
- 2 rounded tablespoons icing sugar

Pre-heat the oven to 140°C/275°F/ Gas 1

Split the vanilla pod lengthways, scrape out the seeds and put in a saucepan with the cream. Heat gently, then stir to spread the seeds throughout the cream. Cover and leave for 30 minutes to infuse. If using vanilla extract, do the same.

Heat the milk in a saucepan and add the chocolate broken into pieces and stir until the chocolate is melted.

In a bowl, beat together the egg yolks and icing sugar. Add the chocolate cream and vanilla milk and beat together until completely combined. Pour through a sieve into small pots or ramekin dishes. (I use small Chinese tea cups).

Line a small baking dish or tin with folded kitchen paper or newspaper (this keeps the pots steady in the bain marie) and place the pots on top. Fill halfway up the pots with boiling water.

Bake in the oven for 45 minutes to 1 hour until slightly puffed and spongy to the touch, and a slight crust has formed on top. (Don't worry that they are overcooked as a crust is necessary for when they have cooled.)

Allow to cool, then chill in the fridge for 8 hours, or preferably overnight.

This chocolate pot is like chocolate clotted cream. Under the crust will be a glossy cream of thick unctuous richness. Not many people can eat two!!

I first cooked this after a pregnant friend expressed a longing for chocolate mousse as she couldn't eat it because of the raw egg.

Sarah P, Able Community Care Gazette Reader, Devon

Bread and Butter Pudding

- ½ pint (275ml) milk
- ⅛ pint (70ml) double cream
- Grated rind of half a small lemon
- 2oz (50g) caster sugar
- 3 eggs
- Pannetone cake
- ½ oz (10g) candied lemon or orange peel finely chopped
- 2oz (50g) currants
- Freshly-grated nutmeg

Heat oven to 180°C/350°F/Gas 4

Butter a 2 pint (1 litre) oblong enamel baking dish.

Slice the Pannetone and butter it. Put one layer on the base of the dish, sprinkle with the candied peel and half the currants. Put another layer of Pannetone in the dish and sprinkle with the rest of the currants.

Put the milk and cream together in a measuring jug, stir in the lemon peel and sugar. Whisk the eggs in a small basin and add to the milk mixture. Pour the whole lot over the Pannetone and sprinkle with freshly grated nutmeg.

Bake in the oven for 30-40 minutes. Serve warm.

This is delicious and provides the perfect solution for what to do with those dry Italian cakes you get given at Christmas!!

Dame Judi Dench

Branson's Bramley Apple Pie

Filling:
- 675g bramley apples
- 75-100g soft brown sugar
- Juice of 1 orange
- 1 teaspoon of mixed spice
- 1 tablespoon plain white flour
- 25g butter

Crust:
- 175g prepared short-crust pastry
- 1-2 teaspoons caster sugar

Pre-heat the oven to 200°C/400°F/Gas 6

Cooking time: 45 minutes

Peel and core the apples, cut into thick slices and set aside. Then mix together the sugar, mixed spice and flour. Place a third of the apple slices in the base of a 1.2 litre deep pie dish and sprinkle with half the sugar mix. Cover with half the remaining apples and sugar then arrange the rest of the apples on top. Finally, pour in the orange juice, cut the butter into small pieces and dot over the apples.

Roll the pastry out to an oblong, on a lightly floured surface about 4cm larger than the pie dish. Cut off a 1.25cm strip. Now dampen the edge of the dish with a little water and place the strip over the edge. Dampen this pastry edge, and then put the pastry lid in position over the top. Press the edges firmly together. Any trimmings you have left over should be used to decorate the top. Finally, brush the pastry with a little water and sprinkle with the caster sugar.

Bake the pie in a pre-heated oven for 15 minutes then reduce temperature to 180°C/350°F/Gas 4 and cook for 30 minutes or until the pie is golden brown. Finish by sprinkling with a little more sugar after baking.

After a busy time travelling the world managing his empire and relaxing on Necker, Sir Richard likes nothing more than coming back to a home-cooked meal; and what better pudding is there than this classic?

Sir Richard Branson

www.uk.virginmoney.com

Canterbury Tart

For the pastry:
- 335g plain flour
- 200g unsalted butter
- 200g icing sugar, sieved
- 1 egg
- 1 egg yolk

For the filling:
- 6 eggs
- 375g caster sugar
- 3 lemons, zested and juiced
- 185g butter, melted
- 3 cooking apples, grated
- 2 red apples, sliced into thin strips

Pastry:

Cream the butter and icing sugar together until pale.

Add the flour and crumble until resembles fine breadcrumbs.

Add the egg and yolk, mix until a smooth paste then refrigerate for half an hour.

Once chilled, roll out to 4mm thickness to line a 10" flan case. Blind-bake at 150°C for 10-15 minutes or until the pastry starts to colour.

Take out of the oven and leave to cool whilst making the filling.

Filling:

In a bowl, beat together the eggs, sugar and lemon zest and juice.

Pour the melted butter into the egg mix whilst using a whisk to stir.

Mix in the grated cooking apples and pour into the prepared pastry case.

Place the sliced red apples neatly on top of the egg mix to form a circular pattern and bake at 150°C for 40-45 minutes until when nudged the centre slightly wobbles.

Best served with crème fraîche and raspberry coulis.

A real favourite

Jessica Simpson,
Pastry Chef,
Metfield Bakery
www.metfieldbakery.com

Chris Bailey's Pear Dessert

- 8 blush pears
- 2 bottles ginger wine
- Tub of mixed peel
- Selection of dried fruit, nuts, toasted almond flakes
- Butter
- Honey
- Mascarpone
- Crème fraîche

Peel the pears, place in a saucepan with the ginger wine and cook. Bring to the boil and cook till soft. Leave overnight if possible to allow the pear to soak up the wine.

To prepare the base, place a small knob of butter in the frying pan, add the mixed cut peel, diced dried fruit, almond flakes, crushed nuts – whatever you fancy preparing for your guests as the attachment to the pears.

Cook till warm, add honey and stir.

Create this mix as your base on the plate, placing the pear on top.

Mix the crème fraîche and mascarpone together to add on the plate next to the pear.

This is a dish that I often serve to dinner party guests – it's easy to pre-prepare, not too filling, sweet and delicious to end a meal.

Chris Bailey, Event Management Services

www.ems4events.co.uk

Clootie Dumpling

You will need a piece of white cotton or linen, soaked and wrung out in hot water, then sprinkled with flour to make a seal.

- 2 cups sugar
- 1lb self-raising flour
- $\frac{1}{4}$ lb suet
- $\frac{3}{4}$ lb raisins
- $\frac{1}{2}$ lb currants, sultanas
- 1 grated apple
- 1 cup milk
- 1 tablespoon black treacle
- 1 teaspoon cinnamon
- 1 teaspoon mixed spice

Have a good sized pan, half-filled with boiling water on the stove.

Mix all the ingredients in a bowl and mix into a ball. Put onto the floured cloth and tie with string, leaving some space for the dumpling to swell.

Put a plate in the pan and boil dumpling for $3\frac{1}{2}$ hours, topping up with boiling water as required.

Remove from pan and undo string and place dumpling onto an ovenproof plate. Put the dumpling in a moderate over for 10 minutes. This gives the dumpling a nice skin. It can then be served sliced up with custard, butter, jam or cream. Any leftovers can be fried or toasted but it is nice even to eat cold.

I used to go to my Grandmother's farm in the hills of Perthshire for holidays etc. If one of my family's birthdays fell on one of the days we were there, she didn't bake a cake (although she was a fabulous baker and made her own bread etc). She made this special Clootie Dumpling. I managed to get the recipe from her and I hope anyone who makes it will enjoy!

Kate Boyd, Glasgow, Able Community Care Gazette Reader

Christmas Orange

Take one orange and cut it in half.

Extract the pith and the juice.

Mix the extracts with a jelly and fill the halves of orange with the mixture.

When setting, place a piece of banana in the centre of each orange. When firmly set, place a cherry on top of the banana.

At a certain time in my life a hand of authority touched my shoulder and the owner's voice said "You are travelling a long distance – immediately". At this stage I said "Goodbye" to my wife and my 6 year old son, not knowing how long my absence would be. Travelling involved leaving Heathrow by air, at midnight, and after many hours of stopping and starting, we arrived at a location in the Pacific where the climate was the exact opposite I had just left; It was like an oven.

However, at this location, after many rehearsals over a period of time, we were instructed on how to welcome the detonation of a nuclear war-head. "Listen carefully to the exact time of 10 to 1 seconds when the explosion would occur" Having turned our bodies to it, to protect our eyes, our fists having been screwed tightly together, pressed into our eye sockets, as protection from the brilliance of the nuclear flash, despite eyes being covered, the skeleton of our hands was clearly visible. The warmth from the unspecified height of the explosion on my back would have been more comfortable had it been from a different source.

After the explosion came the blast, following after minutes of silence, and we were allowed to turn round to observe the much vaunted mushroom cloud surrounding the menacing fire-storm. – in short – the abuse of the planet's natural atmosphere and resources.

My first thought at the moment, having in mind the political situation at that time was "What have we done to bring an innocent child into a world of this calibre?" My second thought was that the site of this experiment was Christmas Island. Happy Christmas?

Dennis H, Toftwood

Earl Grey Tea Mousse

- 300g milk
- 50g sugar
- 3 egg yolks
- 2 earl grey tea bags
- Gelatine
- 500g cream
- 75g condensed milk

Boil the milk and tea together and add to the eggs and sugar that have been mixed. Pour back into the pan and cook on a low heat stirring all the time. The mixture will start to thicken. Take off the heat at 82°C and strain.

Add 3 leaves of gelatine that have been soaked in cold water.

Allow to cool. Then fold in 300g of whipped cream and pour into tea cups filling ¾ full. Put in the fridge and allow to set. To finish, half-whip 200g cream and 75g condensed milk and spoon onto the mousse.

Serve on a saucer with some shortbread biscuits.

 *Delicate and Different!*

Kevin and Jacki Mangeolles,
The Neptune Restaurant with Rooms,
Hunstanton

www.theneptune.co.uk

Joan Collins' Festive Christmas Egg Nog

In blender:

- 2oz Rum
- 2oz Brandy
- 2oz Kahlua
- 4 large scoops of vanilla ice cream – in freezer
- Add milk and cream to taste

Blend up until foamy.

You can obviously double or triple this recipe – Try one first and see how it tastes.

Guaranteed to restore holiday cheer!!

Joan Collins OBE

Favourites Pudding

Slice your favourite sponge cake and arrange in your favourite dish.

Smear with your favourite jam and optional berries in season.

Pour over your favourite melted ice cream to moisten the pudding.

Keep for a couple of hours in the fridge and serve to your favourite guests.

A favourite!

Sir Ian Mckellen

High Octane Rice Pudding

You will need :-

- Large mug (250g) of pudding rice
- A tin (410g) of evaporated milk
- 2 large tablespoons of golden syrup
- 1 large tablespoon of caster or brown sugar
- 5 heaped teaspoons of unsalted butter
- Up to one pint of whole milk (semi-skimmed will do)
- And lots of grated nutmeg according to taste

This recipe for rice pudding is tweakable depending on your taste. If you like your rice puddings runny, then you use a whole pint of milk. If you like it thicker then just use a $\frac{1}{3}$ of a pint or you can use any amount between to two. I like mine really thick so that when it is cold you can cut it into slabs like flapjack and it has almost the same calorific content as Kendal Mint Cake. So here is my rice pudding recipe.

Put the rice into a pan of cold water and bring to the boil. Sieve and rinse and place in a large baking dish.

Stir in the syrup and sugar and then pour in the evaporate milk and continue stirring.

Add as much milk as required but at least a $\frac{1}{3}$ of a pint but not more than a pint and continue stirring.

Put a large teaspoon of butter in each corner of the dish and one in the middle.

Add a liberal sprinkling of nutmeg (I like to use a lot – at least two teaspoons). At this point you can let the pudding for several hours until you are ready to cook it or you can put it straight in the oven.
I have a gas oven which is either off or on full and it normally takes around 50 minutes on the full setting. If you leave it for a few minutes longer you will get that lovely thick leathery crust on the surface. (Delegate somebody else to do the washing up!!).

The pudding can be eaten straight from the oven or if refrigerated overnight the next day.

Having travelled around the world for the last 30 years and eaten everything from spiders and grubs to armadillos, rats, rattlesnakes, bats and pythons, I thought it only fitting to go for a really exotic dish, so here's my rice pudding. My mum ran an off-licence in Hull and worked seven days a week so the only rice pudding I knew came from a tin. It was my Aunty Doris who introduced me to a proper rice pudding when I was five years old and I ended up arguing with my cousins over the skin and who would scrape out the dish. When it was first out of the oven it was too hot to eat and when I complained I was told to eat it around the outside first. So I promptly got up with my dish from the table and went into the garden!!!

Mike Linley, Producer and Filmmaker

www.hairy-frog.co.uk

Lemon Surprise Pudding

- 2oz (50g) unsalted butter
- 1 large lemon
- 3oz (75g) caster sugar
- 2 large eggs – separated
- 1 dessertspoon plain flour
- ½ pint (300ml) warm milk

Heat the oven to 180°F/Gas 4.

Use a zester to remove the lemon peel and chop finely.

Cream together the butter and sugar until light and fluffy, then beat in the egg yolks until smooth.

Stir in the sifted flour and warmed milk to make a smooth batter.

Add lemon juice and zest. (The lemon juice may lightly curdle the mixture, but don't worry.)

Whisk the egg whites until firm but not too stiff and fold into the mixture.

Turn into a baking dish and bake for about 40-45 minutes until puffed and golden brown.

Serve hot, warm or cold. This pudding is versatile!

Pam Shrimpton, Able Community Care Gazette Reader

Maureen's Pear Turnover Tart

- 10oz plain flour
- 6oz butter or margarine
- 4 tablespoons cold water

Syrup:
- 3oz butter
- 3oz honey
- 1½ oz muscovado sugar
- Ginger and cinnamon (optional)
- 4-6 pears depending on size (Apples, apricots and plums can be used too)

Heat oven to 440°F/Gas 6

Rub together flour and butter/margarine into crumbs.

Mix in water and knead gently. (Pastry can be kept cool in fridge for a few minutes.)

Syrup:

Put butter, honey and sugar in saucepan over gentle heat. Bring to boil for a minute and then turn into a baking tin or dish to coat the base of a large baking tin or dish.

Cut each ¼ pear into 3 and arrange them on top of the syrup - first around the edges of the dish and then fill in the centre. Sprinkle with cinnamon and ginger if liked.

Roll out the pastry a little larger than the baking tin/dish. Lift the pastry over the pears and tuck in all round the edges. Prick the pastry with a fork.

Bake for 30 minutes. Leave to cool for 10-15 minutes.

Serve. Turn onto serving plate so the tart is upside down or right side up with the pears glistening with syrup. Crème fraîche is probably best with this tart.

This is the fastest disappearing pudding I ever make and it is a recipe, borrowed and slightly adapted, from a very old friend and so it bears her name.

Dorothy Reeder,
Reepham

Mango with Sticky Rice

- 1 cup of Thai sweet rice
- 1 large cup of water
- 2 ripe mangos cut into pieces
- 4 tablespoons brown sugar
- 1 can good quality coconut milk
- 1 small spoon salt
- 2 teaspoons coconut flavouring
- 1 teaspoon vanilla essence
- 2 teaspoons of arrowroot powder dissolved in 2 tablespoons water

To prepare the rice:

Soak the rice in 1 cup water for minimum of half an hour and maximum of 4 hours.

Add another $^3/_4$ cup of water plus $^1/_4$ can of coconut milk, $^1/_4$ teaspoon of salt and 1 tablespoon of brown sugar. Stir all into the rice.

Bring to a gentle boil then partially cover with a lid.

Put on medium-low heat. Leave a gap for steam to escape under the saucepan lid. Simmer for 20 minutes, or until the coconut water has been absorbed by the rice.

Turn off the heat, but leave the pot on the burner with the lid on tight.

Allow to sit for 5-10 minutes.

To prepare the sauce:

Warm (do not boil) the rest of the can of coconut milk over medium-low heat for 5 minutes. Add 3 tablespoons of sugar, stirring to dissolve.

Taste the sauce for sweetness, adding more sugar
if desired, remembering that the sweetness will dissolve when added to the rice.

Add scoops of rice directly to the sauce pot and stir over low heat, gently breaking apart large lumps but leaving smaller lumps/chunks.

Add the mango pieces and gently stir until everything is warmed through.

To enjoy:

Divide up equally and make sure everyone has plenty of mango and sauce.

My favourite sweet is without doubt the exquisite Thai dish, Mango with Sticky Rice. It is light, exotic, sexy and natural and this is how you make it.

Humphrey Hawksley,
BBC World Affairs Correspondent

www.humphreyhawksley.com

Mexican Spiced Chocolate Ice Cream

- 1½ oz (50g) good dark chocolate
- 10fl oz (300ml) milk
- 1 teaspoon ground cinnamon
- ½ teaspoon ground ginger
- ¼ teaspoon salt
- 1¼ cups (10oz/275g) sugar
- 3 eggs
- 10fl oz (300ml) double cream
- 2 teaspoons vanilla extract
- ½ teaspoon almond extract

Melt the chocolate in a bowl over boiling water; or in a medium-sized pan over a low heat and stir continuously.

When melted, stir in milk, cinnamon, ginger and salt, increase to a medium heat.

Keep stirring until well blended.

In a mixing bowl, blend together the sugar and eggs to make a thick paste.

Pour this into the milk and chocolate mixture. Cook and stir until it thickens (till it "coats" the back of a wooden spoon). Or the mixture could be left in a bowl over boiling water to cook gently. If this custard mixture gets slightly overcooked and lumpy it may need to be sieved to get a smooth consistency.

Remove from the heat and cool. Place in fridge.

Then add the double cream and pour into a 1.1 litre ice cream maker for 20 minutes or so (or whip the cream and add to the mixture, pour into a plastic container and freeze for 4-6 hours till "mushy" and then beat well and return to the freezer).

You can also add dried fruit, chocolate chips, chopped dried cranberries or chopped nuts before final freezing.

I hardly ever eat puddings! Tasting this ice cream has converted me – it's utterly delicious.

Joanna Lumley OBE

Nutmeg Ice Cream

- 120g sugar
- 3 egg yolks
- 500ml single cream
- 10g cornflour
- 4g nutmeg

Mix the sugar, cornflour & nutmeg in a bowl.

Beat in the egg yolks, then enough cream to make a smooth pouring paste.

Heat the rest of the cream either stirring over a low heat or in a bain marie.

When it gets warm, gently stir in the sugar & egg yolk mixture

Stir continuously until the custard thickens (around 65-70°C) and just coats the back of a spoon.

Don't overheat, though, because at around 85°C you will be cooking everything!

Immediately remove from the heat.

Allow to cool.

Freeze using a domestic ice cream machine.

You can also just cover and place in the freezer, stirring every hour or so.

This is my favourite and goes very well with fruit puddings.

Simon Edye, Ronaldo Ices, Norwich

www.ronaldo-ices.co.uk

Semifreddo di Mandorle

with Kumquat Compote

For the praline:
- 6oz (175g) caster sugar
- 6oz (175g) whole almonds skins on

For the semifreddo:
- 15fl oz (425ml) double cream, thoroughly chilled
- 4½ oz (125g) caster sugar
- 4 large eggs separated

For the compote:
- 1lb (450g) kumquats
- 9oz (250g) caster sugar

You will also need a large baking sheet, lightly oiled and a loaf tin lined with double thickness cling film.

To make the praline:

Put the sugar and almonds in a heavy based pan and place over a low heat. The sugar will melt – do not stir it.

When the sugar has caramelised and become a deep toffee colour, carefully rotate the pan until all the nuts are covered with caramel.

When nuts begin to pop, pour the praline on to the prepared baking sheet and spread out using a palette knife.

Leave to cool and harden, then crush the praline using a food processor or with a rolling pin, until it is coarse and gritty.

To make the semifreddo:

Whisk the cream and 3oz (75g) sugar together until the mixture forms soft peaks, then refrigerate.

Whisk the egg yolks and remaining sugar in a medium sized glass or stainless steel bowl placed over a pan of gently simmering water making sure the bottom of the bowl doesn't touch the water, Whisk until the mixture is pale, light and fluffy and the whisk leaves a ribbon like trail when lifted out. This will take 3-5 minutes. Remove the bowl from the pan and continue to whisk the mixture until completely cool.

Using a large metal spoon very carefully fold into the chilled whipped cream. Fold in half the crushed praline.

In a glass or stainless steel bowl, whisk egg whites until they reach the stiff peak stage. Mix 1 tablespoon of the whisked egg whites into the cream to loosen it slightly. Then gently fold in remaining egg whites and rest of the praline. Pour the mixture into the loaf tin, cover and freeze over night.

Meanwhile make the kumquat compote. Slice each kumquat horizontally into 3-4 slices, then remove and discard any pips. Place the kumquat slices in a medium sized pan with sugar and 12fl oz of water and bring to the boil, reduce heat, cover and simmer for 30 minutes or until fruit is tender. Cool, transfer to a lidded container and chill until needed.

I love all things Italian, so even the name of this recipe is wonderful to say, as is the taste.

Although a bit fiddly it can be made days ahead so is ideal for an easy dinner party pudding. The kumquats are seasonal, only available in Autumn, which I hadn't realised when I had friends scouring Norfolk to find kumquats. A raspberry coulis can be used instead of kumquats.

Jackie Chipping,
Norfolk

Spiced Apple and Raisin Crumble

- 2lb Bramley apples, peeled and sliced
- 1oz soft brown sugar
- $\frac{1}{4}$ teaspoon ground cloves
- 1 level teaspoon ground cinnamon
- 3oz raisins
- 2 tablespoons water

For the crumble:

- 8oz plain or wholewheat flour
- 5oz soft brown sugar
- 3oz butter at room temperature
- 1 level teaspoon baking powder

Pre-heat oven to, 180°C/350°F/Gas 4

Use a 3pt (1.75 litre) pie dish

Place the sliced apples, raisins, 1oz sugar and spices in a saucepan. Sprinkle with the water and then cook gently until the apples are soft and fluffy. Spoon the mixture into the pie dish and sprinkle with the crumble topping and then bake in the oven till golden brown.

To make crumble topping:

Place the flour in a large mixing bowl, sprinkle in the baking powder and then add the butter and rub it into the flour lightly, using your finger-tips. Then when it all looks crumbly, and the fat has been dispersed fairly evenly, add the sugar and combine well.

I really enjoy simple old-fashioned puddings and a crumble is my favourite.

Nicholas Parsons OBE

St Clement's Cheesecake

- 2 large packets Philadelphia cheese
- 1 tin of condensed milk
- Fresh oranges and lemons
- 9oz digestive biscuits
- 3oz butter

Place the digestive biscuits in a freezer bag and crush with a rolling pin.

Melt the butter over a low heat and mix in the crushed biscuits (NB you **must** use butter and not margarine!).

Place the mixture in a flan dish, smooth down with the back of a spoon and place in the fridge. Leave until the mixture has set.

Mix the Philadelphia cheese and condensed milk in a bowl. Slowly mix in the juice of freshly squeezed oranges and lemons to sharpen the taste without allowing the mixture to become runny.

Spread the mixture over the set biscuit base and return to the fridge until the mixture is set. Then serve and enjoy!

This is one of my favourite recipes.

Richard Bacon MP for South Norfolk

www.richardbacon.org.uk

Steamed Syrup Sponge

- 150g caster sugar
- 150g margarine or butter
- 150g self-raising flour
- 25g cornflour
- 3 eggs
- 6 dessertspoons of syrup
- ½ teaspoon vanilla essence

Grease a 2 pint (1 litre) pudding basin and add about 6 dessertspoons of syrup.

Cream the fat and sugar, add the vanilla essence and eggs and beat until pale and fluffy. Slowly fold in sieved flour and cornflour. Adjust the mixture if necessary to achieve a "dropping consistency" and add to the syrup in the pudding basin. Cover with greaseproof paper, then loosely with tin foil. Then place the basin in a saucepan with water coming about two thirds up the basin. Put the lid on the saucepan and simmer gently for about 1½ hours, checking occasionally to make sure all the water has not evaporated.

This recipe has been a favourite of family and friends for four generations, so is well tried and tested. It can be varied by adding 2 teaspoons of ground ginger, or omitting the syrup and adding 50g cocoa powder or 50g dried fruit and all forms freeze well once cooked.

Trish Lawrence,
Swanton Morley

Sticky Toffee Pudding

For the cake:

- 100g dark muscovado sugar
- 175g self-raising flour
- 125ml full-fat milk
- 1 egg
- 1 teaspoon vanilla extract
- 50g unsalted butter, melted
- 200g chopped, rolled dates

For the sauce:

- 200g dark muscovado sugar
- 25g unsalted butter in little blobs
- 500ml boiling water

Serves 4-6

Pre-heat the oven to 190°C/Gas 5 and butter a 1½ litre pudding dish.

Combine the 100g muscovado sugar with the flour in a large bowl.

Pour the milk into a measuring jug, beat in the egg, vanilla and melted butter and then pour this mixture over the sugar and flour, stirring with a wooden spoon to combine.

Fold in the dates, then scrape into the prepared pudding dish. Don't worry if it doesn't look very full. It will expand.

Sprinkle over the 200g dark muscovado sugar and dot with the butter. Pour over the boiling water (Yes Really!!) and transfer to the oven. Cook for 45 minutes (though the pudding might need 5-10 minutes more).

The top of the pudding should be springy and spongy when it's cooked; underneath the butter, sugar and boiling water will have turned into a rich, sticky sauce. Serve with ice-cream, crème fraîche or cream.

I cannot claim this as my own creation, but I can say it is absolutely delicious and very easy to do. Unfortunately my waistline tells you all you need to know about the quality of this dish!

Simon Newbery, Orchard Toys. Wymondham

www.orchardtoys.com

125

The Best
Crème Brulée

- 750mls pure cream
- 1 tablespoon castor sugar
- 1 teaspoon vanilla essence
- 6 egg yolks
- 2 tablespoons brown sugar

Beat yolks and sugar till combined but not for too long. Bring cream to almost boil and add vanilla, yolks and sugar mix. Pour into oven proof soufflé dishes till almost to top. Put soufflé dishes into a baking tray and pour 2 inches of water into tray. This will allow brulée to cook slowly. Cook in oven on 170° for 35-40 minutes or till firm when shaken.

Cool then place in fridge. Just before serving sprinkle brown sugar on top and put under grill till caramelised. Cool. Then serve with fresh cream and berries.

The Best Creme Brulée came about when I was an apprentice working in a very male dominant kitchen only to end up in tears 4 days out of 5. The chefs were mainly French and they did know how to cook, so I gathered as many recipes and methods as I could. This one is a real winner.

My dad was a pastry chef/ baker and this is where the passion for cooking came from. Now my daughter at 13 loves cooking and is extremely imaginative with food as well. BUT I have suggested to have cooking as a hobby as it's a very demanding job. But if it gets in your blood it's very hard to remove.

When I visit Norwich again I'd love to cook this dish for you.

Jo Martin, Gold Coast, Australia

Trifle

- 6 sponge trifle cakes
- Good quality raspberry jam
- 2-3fl oz sweet sherry
- 10oz fresh or frozen raspberries
- 1oz sugar
- 4 egg yolks
- 12fl oz cream, $\frac{1}{2}$ double, $\frac{1}{2}$ single
- 8 drops of pure vanilla essence
- Rounded teaspoon of either cornflour or custard powder
- 10fl oz double cream

Cut the trifle sponges in half lengthwise. Spread with jam and cut each into 8.

Place in glass trifle dish. Sprinkle over sherry, warm raspberries (until sugar dissolves) – do not boil or overcook. Place on top of soaked trifle sponges. Make custard. Blend egg yolks with cornflour or custard powder and vanilla essence (no lumps). Heat cream until hot, not boiling. Whisk into egg mixture and return to heat to thicken. Cool and then pour over the trifle. If doesn't matter if the layers are not separate – it's nicer when they run into each other. Whisk the double cream until floppy and just holds its shape. Place on top of the trifle. Swirl around and place cling film on top. Place in fridge.

Before serving, place either cherries and angelica or halved blanched almonds lightly grilled on top of the trifle.

A proper traditional trifle and perfect at any time!

Jane Holl, Sparham

The Amazing Eggless Sugarless Fatless Cake

- 8oz cooking dates
- 10fl oz water
- 1lb mixed dried fruit
- 3 teaspoons baking powder
- 6oz plain flour
- Grated rind of 1 orange
- 1 teaspoon mixed spice
- $3\frac{1}{2}$ oz chopped walnuts

Oven 180°C

Put dates and water into a saucepan, heat gently until dates are soft, remove from heat and mash to break up dates.

Mix all the other ingredients in a large bowl, mix in the dates.

Spoon into a greased and lined 2lb loaf tin and level the top.

Bake for $1\frac{1}{4}$ -$1\frac{1}{2}$ hours until a skewer comes out clean.

Cool and serve in slices.

Amazing indeed!

Caroline Scott, Able Community Care

Banana Cakes

Cakes:
- 3½ oz (90g) butter, softened
- 2 ripe bananas, mashed
- 1 egg, beaten
- 3fl oz (85ml) milk
- 1 tablespoon runny honey
- 7oz (200g) self-raising wholemeal flour
- ¼ teaspoon baking powder
- 3½ oz (90g) sultanas

Icing: (optional)
- 4½ oz cream cheese
- 1 tablespoon runny honey
- 1 teaspoon lemon or orange juice

Makes 12 fairy cakes/muffins

Pre-heat oven to
180°C/350°F/Gas 4

Line bun/muffin tray with paper cake cases.

Cream together the butter and bananas.

Mix in the egg, honey and milk.

Gently fold in the flour, baking powder and sultanas.

Divide the mixture between the paper cases and bake for 15 minutes, or until they are golden in colour.

Cool before decorating.

To make the icing mix all the ingredients together to make a smooth paste and spread a little on each cake. Yum Yum!!

These banana cakes are really easy and fun to make with my two boys and as they contain no added sugar and lots of fruit, they are quite healthy too.

Becky Jago,
Anglia Television

Banana Loaf

- 2 cups plain flour
- $1\frac{1}{4}$ teaspoons baking soda
- Pinch of salt
- 2 eggs (beaten)
- $\frac{1}{2}$ cup butter
- $\frac{1}{2}$ cup sugar
- 2 cups of mashed overripe bananas
- $\frac{1}{2}$ cup vanilla yoghurt
- 1 teaspoon vanilla

Topping: (optional)
- Sliced banana
- $\frac{1}{2}$ teaspoon cinnamon
- $\frac{1}{2}$ teaspoon sugar

Pre-heat the oven to 350°F. Grease and flour a loaf pan.

Cream together the butter and sugar. Add the eggs, vanilla, yoghurt and the mashed bananas and mix well.

Slowly stir in the flour, adding a little at a time. Then mix in the baking soda and salt, mixing thoroughly.

Pour the mixture into your prepared loaf pan. If the mixture is too stiff to pour you may want to add a little more yoghurt and mix well until you reach the desired consistency. Only mix a little yoghurt at a time to avoid making the mixture too runny.

(Optional) Place banana slices on top of the mixture in the loaf pan and then sprinkle with cinnamon and sugar.

Bake in the centre of the oven for around 60 minutes. Oven times may vary, so check to see if the loaf is ready by inserting a knife or toothpick into the centre of the loaf. It should come out completely clean when ready.

Allow to cool in the loaf pan for 10 minutes before placing on a wire rack to cool fully.

This is really good.

I chose this recipe because it is delicious, healthy and easy. My 19 year old son bakes it for the house!

Caroline Richardson, General Manager, The Norwich Playhouse

www.norwichplayhouse.org

The Best Chocolate Cake in the World

- 350g good quality chocolate
- 5 eggs
- 300g sugar
- 225g butter
- 125ml water

Melt the chocolate, butter and two-thirds of the sugar in a pan with the water to make a syrup.

Add the remaining sugar to the eggs and whisk until three times the original volume.

Fold the chocolate mix into the egg mix.

Pour the mixture into a greaseproof, lined tray and bake at 170°C for approximately 40 minutes.

This is our best-selling dessert on the current menu, so it must be good!

It's also great for gluten-free diets.

Tim Abbott, The Pigs, Edgefield

www.thepigs.org.uk

Boiled Cake Recipe

- 8oz self-raising flour
- 12oz mixed fruit
- 4oz margarine or butter
- 3 beaten eggs
- 4oz sugar
- ¼ pint water

Boiling instructions:

Put fruit, sugar, margarine and water in a saucepan and simmer for 20 minutes.

Allow to cool. Add 3 beaten eggs and stir in flour.

Turn into greased 6" tin and bake in very moderate oven 300 – 325°F/150°C for about 90 minutes.

(Place on shelf below middle.) Cool before serving.

A *family favourite.*

Peter and Jose Hosking,
Able Community Care Gazette Readers

Bran Loaf

- 1 measure (I use a mug) of All Bran
- 1 measure of mixed fruit
- 1 measure sugar
- 1 measure milk

Mix together in a bowl and soak for one hour.

Add 1 measure of self-raising flour and mix.

Pour into a greased and/or lined loaf tin (2lb or 2 x 1lb)

Bake at 150°C for 1–1¼ hours.

Check in the middle with a skewer to ensure it's cooked through.

This loaf is very moist, keeps for ages, freezes well and no scales are needed.

This cake is lovely for afternoon tea with or without butter. I make it frequently for anyone who has a lazy bowel!!!

Chrissie Heaps-Campbell, Able Community Care

Chocolate Brownies

Yummy gooey chocolate brownies with a twist (suitable for wheat-free and gluten-free diets).

- 175g of good-quality dark chocolate
- 200g of unsalted butter
- 200g of golden caster sugar
- 3 medium eggs
- Half a teaspoon of chilli powder (depending on taste)
- 150g of ground almonds
- 50g of pecans or hazelnuts, chopped
- 50g of dried cranberries
- 50g of white chocolate, chopped

Melt the dark chocolate and the butter together. Best done in a saucepan over a gentle heat, but you can do it in the microwave if you're very careful! Once melted, remove from the heat and stir in the sugar.

Let the mixture cool slightly.

Beat the eggs into the mixture, followed by the ground almonds and the chilli powder. Then stir in the white chocolate, the nuts and the cranberries.

Put the mixture into a square 24cm/9in baking tin and bake at 170°C/Gas 3 for about 30 minutes. Makes about 16 brownies. Cut into squares when they've cooled sufficiently.

These are gooey brownies, not suitable for the lunchbox! Serve with ice-cream for a pudding.

If you're feeling particularly decadent, pour some cream liqueur over them as well and curl up with a good book or a soppy film.

Jeannette Flemons, Women's Employment Enterprise Training Unit (WEETU)

www.weetu.org

Chocolate & Coconut squares

- 100g plain chocolate, grated
- 100g soft margarine
- 200g caster sugar
- 2 eggs, beaten
- 200g desiccated coconut
- 50g glacé cherries, chopped

Line a 17.5cm square tin with foil.

Heat oven to 350°F/180°C/Gas 4.

Sprinkle the chocolate into the tin to cover the base evenly.

Cream sugar, margarine until soft. Mix in the egg, coconut and cherries. Spread gently over the chocolate. Bake for 40 minutes until brown. Cool completely before turning out and peeling off the foil. Cut into 12.

They don't hang around long!

Marjorie Eade, Director,
Financial Industry Group, Norwich

www.fignorfolk.com

Fig and Pumpkin Seed Bars

- 60g walnut halves
- 70g soft-dried figs
- 40g sour cherries
- 30g pumpkin seeds
- 200g porridge or rolled oats
- 35g ground almonds
- 100g butter
- 100ml maple syrup
- 90g caster sugar

You will also need a non-stick baking tin, about 24cm square.

Set the oven at 160°C/Gas 4.

Roughly chop the walnuts, figs, cherries and pumpkin seeds. This is done in seconds in a food processor, or longer by hand. The rougher the mix, the more crumbly the biscuits.

Tip in the porridge oats and almonds. Melt the butter in a saucepan, pour in the maple syrup and add the caster sugar. When it gets to a rolling boil, tip in the dry ingredients, stir and tip into the baking tin. Press the mixture down firmly then bake for 20-25 minutes.

Press bars down firmly as they cool. Cut into 12 bars while warm and leave to cool.

Herewith is a favourite recipe devised by the inimitable Nigel Slater. I love it because it's very quick and easy but utterly delicious. I also like to kid myself it's frightfully healthy, because of the figs and nuts, even though it does contain some slightly naughty ingredients!!

Carol Bundock, Senior Broadcast Journalist, BBC Look East

Chunky Apple Walnut Cake

One 10-inch cake:

- 1½ cups vegetable oil
- 2 cups granulated sugar
- 3 eggs
- 2 cups unbleached, all purpose flour, sifted
- ⅛ teaspoon ground cloves
- 1¼ teaspoons ground cinnamon
- ¼ teaspoon ground mace
- 1 teaspoon baking soda
- ¾ teaspoon salt
- 1 cup whole-wheat flour, sifted
- 1¼ cups shelled walnuts, coarsely chopped
- 3¼ cups coarse chunks of peeled Rome Beauty apples
- 3 tablespoons Calvados or applejack

Apple Cider Glaze:

- 4 tablespoons sweet butter
- 2 tablespoons brown sugar
- 6 tablespoons granulated sugar
- 3 tablespoons Calvados or applejack
- 4 tablespoons sweet cider
- 2 tablespoons fresh orange juice
- 2 tablespoons heavy cream

Pre-heat oven to 325°F

Put in large bowl, beat vegetable oil and sugar until thick and opaque. Add eggs, one at a time, beating well after each addition.

Sift together all purpose flour, cloves, cinnamon, mace, baking soda and salt and then stir in whole-wheat flour. Add to oil and egg mixture and mix until well blended.

Add walnuts, apple chunks and Calvados all at once and stir batter until pieces are evenly distributed.

Pour batter into a greased 10 inch round cake pan. Bake for 1 hour and 15 minutes, or until a cake tester inserted in the centre comes out clean.

Let cake rest for 10 minutes and then unmold.

Glaze:

Melt butter in a small saucepan and stir in both sugars. Add remaining ingredients, stir and bring to a boil. Reduce head slightly and cook for 4 minutes. Remove from heat and cool slightly. Pour while still warm over warm cake.

Dark, moist and chunky, with a dream of a glaze.

Felicity Kendal CBE

Ginger Cake

- 4oz (110g) margarine
- 2oz (50g) golden syrup
- 8oz (225g) plain flour
- 2oz (50g) soft brown sugar
- 2 large eggs beaten
- 2 level teaspoons ground ginger
- 6oz (175g) black treacle
- ¼ pint milk
- ½ level teaspoon bicarbonate of soda
- ½ level teaspoon mixed spice
- ½ level teaspoon ground cloves

Turn oven to set at low at 180°C/350°F. Grease an 8 inch square tin.

Warm margarine, treacle, syrup and milk etc in a pan until melted. Do not boil.

Cool.

Meanwhile sift flour, bicarbonate of soda and spices etc into a bowl.

Stir in brown sugar.

Add eggs to treacle mix, beating the mixture well.

Make a well in the centre of dry ingredients. Pour in treacle mixture gradually, beating with a wooden spoon until smooth.

Turn into the prepared tin and bake for 1 hour or until firm.

Cool on a wire rack. Peel off paper when cake is cold.

Never known to fail!

**Maureen Jenkins,
Able Community Care**

Flourless Air Cake

- 250g best quality bittersweet or semi-sweet chocolate, coarsely chopped (or a little bit of milk chocolate if you don't want it too rich.
- 125g unsalted butter, cut into pieces, softened
- 6 large eggs: 2 whole, 4 separated
- 175g sugar
- 2 tablespoons of cognac or Grand Marnier (optional)
- Grated zest of 1 orange (optional)

Whipped cream topping:
- 500ml heavy cream, well chilled
- 3 tablespoons confectioner's sugar
- 1 teaspoon pure vanilla extract (or cointreau!)
- Unsweetened cocoa powder, for sprinkling

Oven: 350°F. Bake time: 35-40 minutes.

Pre-heat the oven. Line the bottom of pan with a round of wax paper; do not butter the pan.

Melt the chocolate in a bowl set over hot water. Remove from the heat and whisk in the butter until melted; set aside.

In a bowl, whisk the 2 whole eggs and the 4 egg yolks with ½ cup of the sugar just until blended. Whisk in the warm chocolate mixture. Whisk in the optional cognac or Grand Marnier and the optional orange zest. In another bowl, with an electric mixer, beat the 4 egg whites until foamy. Gradually add the remaining ½ cup sugar and beat until the whites form soft mounds that hold their shape but are not quite stiff. Stir about ¼ of the beaten egg whites into the chocolate mixture to lighten it; gently fold in the remaining whites. Pour the batter into the pan; smooth the top.

Bake until the top of the cake is puffed and cracked and the centre is no longer wobbly. Do not over bake.

Cool the cake in the pan on a wire rack; the cake will sink as it cools, forming a crater with high sides.

At serving time, whip the cream with the confectioners' sugar and vanilla until not quite stiff. With a spatula, carefully fill the crater of the cake with the whipped cream, pushing it gently to the edges. Dust the top lightly with cocoa powder.

Run the tip of a knife around the edges of the cake; carefully remove the sides of the pan and serve.

Chocolate "Air" cake recipe yields 8 to 12 servings.

Irresistible!

Sophie and Roderick Gordon, Norfolk

www.tunnelsthebook.com

Honey Buns

- 2 eggs
- 75g caster sugar
- 1 teaspoon soft dark sugar
- Pinch salt
- 90g self raising flour
- 1 teaspoon baking powder
- 90g melted butter – cooled
- 1 tablespoon honey

Whisk together the eggs and sugars.

Fold in the sifted flour, baking powder and salt.

Leave the mixture to rest for 30 minutes.

Stir in the melted butter and honey.

Bake in cases, approximately 25 minutes at 180°C/Gas 6.

I would like to contribute the following which my sister makes for me when I have been good.

Stephen Fry, Norfolk

Julie's Chocolate Brownies

- 345g caster sugar
- 80g cocoa powder
- 60g flour
- 1 teaspoon baking powder
- 4 eggs
- 200g chocolate drops
- 200g butter
- 2 teaspoons vanilla essence

Mix all the dry ingredients (except the chocolate drops) together.

Then add all the wet ingredients.

Lastly add the chocolate drops.

Cook at 160°C for 45 minutes to 1 hour until springy to the touch. Remove and leave to cool on a wire rack.

I got this recipe from one of my fellow mums when I had Alice. They are incredibly easy to make and a firm favourite in the Martinsen household. The kids love helping to bake them – and most importantly the ritual of licking the bowl afterwards. I usually freeze some squares, meaning that if anyone comes round I can quickly get them out and hey-presto some coffee and cake to hand! It's also delicious served with ice cream as a dessert.

Claire Martinsen,
Breckland Orchard, Watton

www.brecklandorchard.co.uk

Magic Meg's Starburst Biscuits

To make them Magical you will need:

- 4oz icing sugar
- 8oz butter
- 10oz self raising flour
- 2oz ground almonds
- Star shaped pastry cutters
- Extra icing for decorating
- *Edible glitter (optional)
- Magic Wand (optional)

Mix the flour, the almonds and the icing sugar together.

Then rub in the butter using the tips of your fingers to create a lovely ball of dough. Roll to $\frac{1}{2}$ inch thick on a floured board.

Use star-shaped pastry cutters (if possible) to create star shapes and place on a greased baking sheet. Use the leftover bits to create little tiny balls of dough in different sizes.

Bake in moderate oven until golden brown and remove to cool.

Whilst cooling wave magic wand over star biscuits and little starburst balls and make a special magic spell.

Decorate with a dusting of icing sugar and then a dusting of edible glitter!

*Arrange on a special (preferably sparkly) plate..........
eat, enjoy and may your wish come true!*

Lucy Loveheart, Artist, Norfolk

www.lucyloveheart.com

*Edible glitter available from Ed Able Arts 01388 816309

Nanaimo Bars

Bottom Layer:
- ½ cup unsalted butter
- ¼ cup sugar
- 5 tablespoons cocoa
- 1 egg beaten
- 1¼ cups graham wafer crumbs (if these can't be found the closest would be crushed digestive biscuits)
- ½ cup finely chopped almonds
- 1 cup coconut

Second Layer:
- ½ cup unsalted butter
- 2 tablespoons and 2 teaspoons cream
- 2 tablespoons custard powder
- 2 cups icing sugar

Third Layer:
- 4 squares semi-sweet chocolate (1oz each)
- 2 tablespoons unsalted butter

Bottom Layer:
Melt first 3 ingredients in top of double boiler. Add egg and stir to cook and thicken. Remove from heat. Stir in crumbs, coconut and nuts. Press firmly into an un-greased 8" pan.

Second Layer:
Cream butter, cream, custard powder and icing sugar together well. Beat until light. Spread over bottom layer.

Third Layer:
Melt chocolate and butter over low heat. Cool. Once cool, but still liquid, pour over second layer and chill in fridge. When chilled cut into squares with a hot knife.

This recipe was made famous, in B.C. Canada, by someone entering a local competition in Nanaimo, which is on the east coast of Vancouver Island. They're traditionally made at Christmas time but are fab any time and are particularly more-ish, Enjoy!

Vicky Harvey, Able Community Care

Raisin Shortbread

- 9oz plain flour
- 6oz butter room temperature
- 6oz caster sugar
- 6oz raisins soaked overnight in orange juice

Mix flour, sugar & butter together.

Roll out half the mixture onto a lightly floured & greased dish.

Drain raisins and place on top.

Place the other half of the mixture on top of the raisins.

Crimp the edges and bake in a moderate oven for 20-25 minutes until golden.

Eat hot or cold.

I'm originally from Scotland and this is a Scottish recipe. Once you've tried these you'll be eating them all day long....

John Kelly, Chef, Darby's Freehouse, Swanton Morley

www.darbysfreehouse.com

The Park Charity Café Parsnip Cake

- 10oz (250g) peeled and grated parsnip
- 2 medium eggs, lightly beaten
- 5fl oz (125ml) good grape seed oil
- 8oz (200g) caster sugar
- 15oz (375g) self raising flour
- $\frac{1}{2}$ teaspoon cinnamon
- $\frac{1}{2}$ teaspoon salt
- Dash of quality vanilla essence

Cream Cheese Icing:
- 12oz (300g) quality cream cheese
- 8oz (200g) icing sugar
- Dash of quality anilla essence

Oven Temperature 180°C/Gas 5

Grease & line a deep 7 inch cake tin and put to one side.

Mix together in a large bowl the eggs and add the oil, whilst whisking. When blended, stir in the caster sugar, grated parsnip & vanilla essence and stir until well combined.

Add the self raising flour, cinnamon & salt stirring well to combine. At this point the cake batter will be very stiff. Do not panic at this point it is supposed to be this stiff.

Place into the lined cake tin and bake for approximately 45 minutes, or until a skewer inserted into the cake comes out clean. Remove from the oven and allow to cool.

Whilst the cake is cooling prepare the icing;

Place all the ingredients into a bowl and mix well until combined, chill for 10 to 15 minutes prior to using.

When the cake is cool, slice across the centre and add a couple of dollops of icing and spread across the cake. Place the lid on top and spread the remainder of the icing over.

Put the kettle on, sit down, make yourself an Earl Grey tea and have a slice of the Parsnip Cake and you will realise just how good life really is.....

■■■ *The original recipe for this cake dates back to the days of Elizabeth the First, when parsnips were dried and used to sweeten dishes, much like sugar beet is today. It is a fantastic cake; more spongy than the popular American Carrot Cake but with the same delicious cream cheese icing. It is a firm favourite in our café, with one customer describing it as 'A cross between the best roast dinner and dessert ever all rolled into a cake!'*

Candi Robertson, Park Charity Café, Bawdeswell

www.charitygiving.co.uk

Scented Rose Geranium Cake
with Cardamom Crème fraîche

For the crème fraîche:
- 10-14 cardamom pods
- 500ml crème fraîche (full or half fat)

For the cake:
- 6-8 rose geranium Leaves
- Butter for greasing
- 4 medium eggs
- 175g caster sugar
- 250g ground almonds

For the syrup:
- 3 rose geranium leaves
- 2 tablespoons rosewater
- 2 tablespoons pale runny honey
- Juice of 1 lemon plus zest

Of mysterious origin, possibly French or Middle Eastern this cake has made people weep with anticipation when I've placed it on the table. I once used its seductive rose flavours to lure a rather gorgeous man to my house for supper. It worked. This cake is not too sweet, wheat-free and quite simply the most grown up dessert I've ever come across. The rose geranium leaves must be of a soft and delicate nature picked straight from the scented pelargonium, 'Attar of Roses'. Lovely to have in any kitchen and worth the investment, the plant costs about £1.70 from a number of herb specialist nurseries (see below). The leaves can be used all year round and can also be left out; the cake is delightful without them. It can be made a day in advance if necessary.

Carefully remove the cardamom seeds from their pods by slicing lengthways from one end to the other and opening them with the tip of the knife. Pound the seeds in a mortar until they are ground and their distinctive scent is released. Add them to the crème fraîche and leave, covered, in the fridge. The longer you leave it the stronger the flavour will be but at least an hour is preferable.

Heat the oven to 190°C/Gas 5.

Snip the rose geranium leaves off the plant at the main stem and remove their stalks. Keep 6-8 whole and keep the others aside for the syrup.

Arrange the clean dry leaves face down in a decorative manner on the removable base of a 22-26cm diameter cake tin that has been well greased with butter. Whisk the eggs together with an electric whisk until frothy and then add the sugar while continuing to whisk until the mixture peaks softly (this can be done by hand with gusto if necessary). Then fold the ground almonds carefully in with a metal spoon. Pour the mixture into the cake tin, taking care to keep the geranium leaves flat beneath the mixture as you pour. Bake in the oven for 45-50 minutes until the cake is golden brown on top and pulling away from the sides. Test in the middle with a skewer; if the tip is clean the cake is done. Leave aside to cool for at least 15 minutes.

Meanwhile, in a small saucepan heat up all the ingredients in the syrup with 8 tablespoons of water and bring to the boil, then simmer until the liquid has reduced to half. Remove from heat.

The cake should now be cool enough to remove by placing a large plate face down over the top and carefully flipping both over. Always a tricky manoeuvre, but if well greased the cake should slip down onto the plate with ease. Remove the tin and centre the cake on the plate.

Pour the hot syrup slowly over the cake allowing time for the liquid to soak into the almond sponge. Let it sit, covered, for at least half an hour or even overnight.

Serve each slice with the cardamom crème fraîche on the side and wait for the tears of joy or the seduction to begin…

© Ptolemy Mann 2007, Textile Artist

www.ptolemymann.com

Sticky Ginger Flapjack

- 5oz butter
- 5oz soft brown sugar
- 6-7 tablespoons golden syrup (depending on degree of stickiness preferred)
- 2 teaspoons ground ginger
- 10oz 'old fashioned' or 'jumbo' porridge oats

Pre-heat oven to 180°C.

Line a 9 inch square baking tin with baking parchment.

In a large saucepan and over a gentle heat melt together butter, sugar, golden syrup and ground ginger until the sugar has dissolved.

Taking the pan off the heat, stir in the porridge oats until coated.

Press the mixture into a tin with the back of a metal spoon, making sure to get the mixture into the corners.

Cook for 20-25 minutes until golden brown.
If using an Aga, cook for 7 minutes in the hot oven, followed by around 18 minutes in the warm oven for a perfect result.

When cool, cut into 9 or 12 squares.

Nearly everyone knows how to make flapjack, but this is really good flapjack. My husband William, who adores gingery, syrupy things, set me the challenge of coming up with a homemade flapjack that was better than that sold in our favourite deli/teashop. I think this is, and it is very sustaining as well as being delicious.

This will keep in an airtight tin for around two weeks, or indeed a whole university term so I am assured by my teenage son.

Hazel Gill, Partner, Leathes Prior Solicitors, Norwich

www.leathesprior.co.uk

Susan's Lemon Drizzle Cake

- 6oz (175g) caster sugar
- 6oz (175g) self raising flour
- 6oz (175g) butter
- 3 medium eggs
- 1 teaspoon baking powder
- Grated zest of 1 lemon
- 2½ fl oz (75ml) milk
- Approximately 6 teaspoons of good zesty lemon curd

Topping:
- Juice of 1 large lemon
- 3 tablespoons granulated sugar
- A few pieces of lemon zest

Pre-heat the oven to 180°C/350°F/Gas 4

Line and grease a 7"- 8" round cake or 2lb loaf tin.

Put all the ingredients for the cake into a processor or whisk well with an electric mixer and pour the batter into the prepared tin. Randomly drop into the mixture 6 spoons of lemon curd and bake for 40-50 minutes and test with a skewer to check it comes out clean.

Turn onto a wire cooling rack. Stir 3 tablespoons of sugar into the remaining lemon juice until dissolved and pour over the cake while still warm. Finish by sprinkling with the zest.

Will be eaten as soon as it's cooked!!

Susan Charles, Able Community Care

Walnut Slice

For the pastry base:
- 8oz self raising flour
- 4oz caster sugar
- 6oz margarine
- Egg yolk or milk

For the topping:
- 2 whites of egg
- 6oz sugar
- ¼ lb broken walnuts

For the pastry base:
Put fat into flour and sugar and using egg or a little milk, mix into a dough which can be spread and pressed into a shallow tin and baked in a moderate over till golden. (I think about 30 minutes but I guess!)

For the topping:
Put ingredients into a pan and bring slowly to the boil, stirring until golden brown and fluffy. Spread cooked pastry base with warmed apricot jam. Pour golden mixture on top and spread evenly. Bake in a moderate oven until golden and biscuity. (Here I guess again!) The topping will look shiny and crisp. 20 minutes should do it. Cut into fingers.

I think it was around 1960 when we found the peerless village of Ardentinny and my brother ran the tin-roofed tea-rooms. It wasn't long before it actually got into the Good Food Guide. Teas were the great events. Here is one of my favourites. We always have it on Fireworks Night.

Phyllida Law, Actress

Bunty's Lemonade

- 3 lemons
- 2lbs 4oz sugar
- 1oz citric acid
- 1oz epsom salts
- ½ oz tartaric acid
- 2 pints boiling water
- 1 pint cold water

(Today tartaric acid is unavailable in the local chemist shops but can be bought on the internet).

Put all dry ingredients into a large bowl.

Grate lemon zest into the bowl.

Pour in the boiling water and stir until everything is dissolved.

Add cold water and leave to cool.

Extract juice from the lemons and when liquid is cold, add juice and stir round.

Strain and bottle.

Dilute to taste when serving.

The lemonade will keep for at least 14 days in a fridge but several months if frozen.

NB The strained zest can be used to flavour a Victoria sponge.

Mrs Bunty Walker, a retired farmer's wife, lived in Church Farm, Ashmanhaugh in the 1960's and 70's. She gave this recipe to my sister who was the Rector's wife of Ashmanhaugh from 1967-78.

My sister gave me the recipe and I have included it in our everyday diet since 1970. I give glasses of it to anyone visiting my home and provide it for the annual luncheon for the West Norfolk Flower Club.

Pam Cross, Abbey Farm, Sandringham Estate

Chocolate Fudge

- 4oz margarine
- 1 tablespoon golden syrup
- 1 tablespoon sugar

Melt all together in saucepan on low heat. Take off heat and stir in $\frac{1}{2}$ lb digestive biscuits rolled and crushed, 1 level tablespoon drinking chocolate, or cocoa if not wanting it to be too sweet.

Put in 7" square tin and spread out.

When cold, melt bar of milk cooking chocolate spread over the mixture in the tin.

Cut into fingers when the chocolate is set.

My children and grandchildren love this!

Aunty Mary, Able Community Care Gazette Reader

Fudge

- 2oz butter
- 2 tablespoons golden syrup
- 1lb sugar
- 1 large tin condensed milk

First put four tablespoons of water and the two ounces of butter into a fairly big pan and heat until the butter melts.

Then add the syrup, condensed milk and sugar. Bring gently to the boil.

Stir the mixture constantly with a wooden spoon to make sure it doesn't stick to the pan, also that the sugar doesn't burn. Keep the fudge boiling for exactly ten minutes.

Take from the cooker and beat with a spoon vigorously until it thickens. Pour into a greased tin. When the fudge is almost set, mark into squares.

I found this following recipe in a Girl Guide diary many years ago when I was a young teenager. Being a big fan of fudge, I couldn't resist giving it a go. It works exceedingly well. It was a great hit with my brothers when I was young and I've found it to be a real winner with my colleagues at BBC Radio Norfolk!

**Maggie Secker, Presenter,
BBC Radio Norfolk**

The Gill-Riley

- 1 measure of Bacardi
- 1 measure of Triple Sec
- 1 measure of Dry Martini
- Half a measure of Grenadine
- Half a measure of Lemon Liqueur
- Quarter measure of Sloe Gin
- Juice of one and half limes

Mix all that lot together in a shaker with crushed ice. Serve in cocktail glasses with a stick that should include a good green olive, a slice of lime and whatever else you feel like bunging on it. This quantity will give you a good drink each. I used to double it up and then spend the early hours doubled-up on the sitting room carpet.

This cocktail was devised whilst undergoing a hedonistic 6 months or so holed up in the cowboy territory of the Suffolk/Norfolk border. Most weekend evenings (and many weekday ones as well) Hazel and I tasked ourselves with 'inventing' (ie something that we had not seen in a book) a cocktail that would match the enjoyment of our favourite cocktail, would include a homemade element and would have a pink tinge. The experiments quite often involved hapless teenage boys; the original name of this mixture – "Filosophy" - was acquired as the result of one such boy. Subsequently Hazel and I agreed we should invent a mixture to celebrate our forthcoming marriage. After some tinkering "Filosophy" became "The Gill-Riley". We are a trifle ambivalent about the name (use of our names, trumpet-blowing etc) but a Gill is a measure of booze and a Riley is an old car dating back to the Cocktail age of the twenties so we have stuck with it.

William Riley, Partner, Leathes Prior Solicitors, Norwich

www.leathesprior.co.uk

Ginger Beer

- 10 pints of boiling water
- One and a quarter pounds of sugar
- 1oz of whole ginger - bruised
- 2 lemons
- $\frac{1}{4}$oz of cream of tartar
- 1oz yeast

Remove the rind off the lemons as thinly as possible.

Strip off all the pith with a very sharp knife.

Cut the lemons into thin slices and put boiling water into an earthenware bowl with the sugar, ginger and cream of tartar and leave until blood heat. Then stir in the yeast.

Cover with a cloth and leave in a warm place for 24 hours.

Skim the yeast from the top of the mixture and then strain the liquid and put into screw top bottles.

In 2 days it should be ready to drink.

A real favourite!

Betty McIver, Able Community Care

Inedible
Delights

Strawberry and Chocolate Cake

- 1 portion of air drying clay
- 12 oven-baked "fimo" strawberries
- A few oven baked "fimo" chocolate shavings
- PVA glue
- 1 tablespoon real semolina
- Cardboard plate

Setting time approximately 6 hours. Cost approx £3.

Take 1 portion of air drying clay and roll into a ball, then shape into your cake shape.

Stick this onto your plate and leave to dry for approximately 6 hours! The cake will still feel spongy to the touch (just like Delia's)!

With a small art paintbrush cover the cake with PVA glue and roll this until completely covered in the semolina. Re-apply a second coat if you'd like a thicker coating.

While you are waiting for this to dry (approximately 15 minutes), make a cup of tea and enjoy with your favourite biscuit!!

Now dab some more PVA onto the top of the cake and sprinkle on the chocolate shavings, piling up towards the centre. Wait another 5 minutes, after which pile on the strawberries, both whole ones and slices.

To preserve this delicious cake you can cover with an acrylic varnish if you wish.

Now sit back and enjoy LOOKING AT – NOT EATING your efforts.

This cake contains: no additives, sugars, salt or fats! And is completely calorific free! Suitable for nut allergies, vegans, colics and dieters!

Denise Ames, Tudor Rose Miniatures, Taverham

www.tudor-rose-miniatures.yolasite.com

This is a non-edible dolls house miniature.

Boiled Cormorant à la Dobson

This is taken from Dobson's pamphlet 'Some Things To Eat In The Bleak Midwinter' (out of print).

This is a splendid and satisfying dish, easy to prepare, highly nutritious, and the enemy of indigestion. First, ensure your kitchen is free of verminous creeping things with hundreds of legs, suckers and antennae. Root them out and exterminate them. Gather the tiny corpses, place them in a paper bag, seal the bag with glue, carry it out of the house, and set fire to it. Do not go back indoors until every last speck has been consumed by the terrible flames. Now, back in the kitchen, take off your windcheater and your big black boots and wash your hands with carbolic soap. Cover your hairstyle, if you have one, with a clean rag fixed in place by an elastic band. You are ready to begin.

Take a freshly-slaughtered cormorant and place it on your work-surface. Vegetarians can substitute the bird with a pretend cormorant modelled in marzipan. I will not remind you of this point again. Pluck all the feathers off and put them in a grinder. Grind them to fine powder, and, using a funnel, pour the powder into a spare cruet. If there is a ring around the cormorant's neck, as there will be if it has been exploited by fisherfolk, carefully remove the ring and throw it away, unless it is old and decorative, in which case you may wish to pop it in an envelope and send it to Antiques Roadshow veteran Hugh Scully. But do that later, on Boxing Day.

Step two. Boil the cormorant.

While the bird is simmering away, prepare the sauce. Chop up into tiny bits four pomegranates, a plum, lots and lots of potatoes, sixteen bananas, another cormorant, some toffee apples and a choc ice. Place the tiny bits in a bowl and stir thoroughly, then get the funnel again and pour the contents of the bowl into the grinder. Adjust the setting to "moderately violent grinding" and switch it on for no more than ten seconds. Transfer back into the bowl. Add water up to the brim and stir. Do not on any account use tap water. You will ruin the recipe and end up with a bowl of inedible sludge unless you use the fantastically pure spring water drawn from the Mysterious Old Well at Pointy Town.

Drain any remaining water from the pan with the boiled cormorant in it, and tip the contents of the bowl in, making sure you do so in one swift movement. Ideally, it should sound like this - *gloop gloop gloop...gloop*. Now put the bowl down somewhere, bring the pan back to the boil and allow to simmer while you fry the cocktail sausages. They should be almost, but not quite, black.

You are nearly done. Take a large oval platter and make a bed of shredded lettuce, chives, spring onions, porridge oats, cream crackers and mayonnaise. Have another look around the kitchen to make sure no creepy-crawlies have appeared from any unhatched eggs you may have overlooked earlier.

Continued over....

Boiled Cormorant
à la Dobson continued

Turn off the heat, and transfer the boiled
cormorant and sauce on to the platter. Use a clean
dishcloth to wipe around the edges in case any of
the sauce is dribbling over the side. Take a Swiss
Army knife out of your pocket, extract the sharpest
blade, and, just in case the last time you used it was
to dislodge a pebble from the sole of your boot,
plunge it into boiling water to sterilise it. Very
carefully slice the blade across the cormorant, as
deep as you can, and put the knife down. Insert the
cocktail sausages into the bird, then sew up the slit
with edible butcher's string.

Try to remember where you left the spare cruet, and
sprinkle the powdered cormorant feathers evenly
over the dish. Add salt and pepper to taste. Serve.

*[Frank Key is the author, podcaster and occasional
performer responsible for Hooting Yard: see
http://hootingyard.org/regarding-mr-key.
He is a UEA graduate and Norwich resident of
about five years' standing, albeit some decades ago.
According to The Guardian [15 November 2007]*

*'Frank Key can probably lay claim to having
written more nonsense than any other man living.'*

Deptford squat stir-fry

from earlier and less informed days of feralism

Ingredients

- Very cheap margarine
- Wheatabix
- Onion
- And the two pilchards from the tin opened at least a week ago, marinating in tomato sauce. Again more would be preferable.

  But maybe Dick or Dave was hungry earlier.

Amounts

what there is

three or four, more if you can find

one, finely chopped

Method

Heat margarine until it almost smells like paraffin.
Add chopped onion, cook till brown almost black.
Now carefully drizzle the crumbled wheatabix into the pan and fry until it's undistinguishable from the onions.
Then scrape mouldy bits (if any) from pilchards and drop the fish avec sauce into the pan.
Cook on gentle heat for five minutes or minuets.
Serve on cold but washed plate.

Better, go to bed hungry

Phil Minton, The Feral Choir

www.philminton.co.uk

Skipper's Delight – A Norfolk Menu

Starters

Coypu Soup with little bits of bread floating on top

(Only when coypu is in season)

Egmere-onaise

Wighton-bait

Fish Course

Yarmouth Kippers

(Specially prepared for us by Scottish fishergirls)

Main Course

Roasted Great Bustard with sprouts, turnips and parsnips

(Only when Great Bustard is available in quantity)

Cromer Shelduck in a nest of fresh samphire, crabsticks and Paston lettuce

(Local advice on cooking Shelduck: "Dew yew put a brick in th'oven along wi' the bird. When the brick is sorft.. so is the shelduck)"

Jugged Ferret

All the above served with Norfolk Dumplings (preferably sinkers) or Stewkey Blues

Dessert

Fair Buttons, flavoured with ginger and served with stewed bullaces

Norfolk Biffin windfalls from Syderstone

Selection of local cheeses including Wendlingdale, Cheddargrave and Mousehold

Sweet Trolley carries Eccles cakes, Hethersett Jellies, Marsham-mallows or Pudding Norton

Beverages

Home brewed Sugar Beet wine

Trunch Punch

Barney Beer

Castle Riesling

Cup O'Cocoa

Coffee and After Nine Mints
(Norfolk people often stay up late)

Toast

Burnt

I am afraid my culinary skills are less than negligible –
I have been known to burn water – but I do feel moved
to play a part.

So I enclose a copy of my idea of a Norfolk menu to
spice up any good local occasion. I hope it's not too long
– but you know what Norfolk people are like once they
sit down and start mardling ...

My menu is based on unbridled delight in anything with
a Norfolk flavour.

Keith Skipper MBE DL